Pier Railways & Tramways

of the British Isles

by
Keith Turner

THE OAKWOOD PRESS

First Edition published 1973
Second Revised Edition published 1999

© Oakwood Press & Keith Turner 1999

British Library Cataloguing in Publication Data
A Record for this book is available from the British Library
ISBN 0 85361 541 1

Typeset by Oakwood Graphics.
Repro by Ford Graphics, Ringwood, Hants.
Printed by The Witney Press, Witney, Oxon.

Acknowledgements

My grateful thanks once again to all those who helped in the research and production of the first edition of this work; without that initial assistance and encouragement the publication of this revised and updated account would never have been possible. I should like also to express my gratitude to those readers of the first edition who took the time to share their memories and special knowledge of these lines with me, and have allowed and enabled me to present that information to a wider audience: thank you.

Front cover: Hythe pier on 28th March, 1959 with a Brush locomotive and its train seen near the pier head station.
Rear cover, top: Ramsey Queen's Pier Tramway in June 1957, the Wickham railcar backs on to her luggage trailer at the pier head.
Rear cover, bottom: Southend pier with one of the 1949 trains. *(All) Colour-Rail*

Published by
The Oakwood Press
P.O. Box 13, Usk, Mon., NP15 1YS.

E-Mail: oakwood-press@dial.pipex.com
Website: http://ds.dial.pipex.com/oakwood-press

Contents

An abiding holiday memory for millions: a train of 1949 electric stock on the Southend pier railway as seen on 14th June, 1970. The line is still operational, though since totally reconstructed.   *T.J. Edgington*

Introduction

There is something enchanting about piers, something doubtless connected with the fact that they create a world of their own halfway between land and sea, where promenaders can see, hear, smell - and in rough weather even touch - the ocean without any risk of shipwreck or sea-sickness. In the Victorian era, when the majority of the British piers were built, the general public was equally fascinated by them and flocked in their thousands to experience these new technological wonders, these mighty ships of wood and iron that could never set sail. (The nautical atmosphere was deliberately enhanced by the naval uniforms of the Pier Master and his crew, resplendent or workaday according to rank.) Some came by pleasure steamer, of which several a day would call at even the humblest pier at the height of the summer season to disgorge their hundreds of passengers, whilst others came by ferry, train, carriage or on foot to play the amusement machines, patronise the kiosks, attend an entertainment in the pavilion, eat, drink and be merry, take the bracing, medically-recommended air, or simply use it as a landing stage to reach their boarding house, hotel or hired villa.

Not everyone wished to - or indeed could - walk the length of some of these leviathans which might stretch the best part of a mile (or even more) out to sea, especially if encumbered with their holiday luggage, and to cater for them the pier railway or tramway was born to supplement - and eventually supersede - other existing forms of conveyance. This book is intended to provide histories of these fascinating, though often little-considered, lines of the British Isles. That is, it deals not with those lines of which a pier housed but one small part, as at a harbour or a ferry port, but with those constructed for the primary purpose of carrying passengers, and their luggage, from one end of a pier to the other. The history of such lines provides an interesting parallel with that of the railway and tramway systems of the rest of the these islands and - if for no other reason - they consequently deserve as much attention as any other minor lines. (A brief account of other types of lines found on British Isles piers is given in Chapter Ten.)

It should perhaps be mentioned here that regardless of its official (or semi-official) title, for the purposes of this book a line has generally been defined as a tramway if it was laid flush with, or on, the pier decking and pedestrians allowed to stroll along it, and as a railway if it was laid on or beside the decking and fenced-off from the rest of the pier for safety reasons (e.g. if a live third rail was used). Similarly, by the term 'pier' is meant a structure of decking on wooden or metal piles, as opposed to the solid forms of jetties, cobs, moles, quays and the like sometimes - misleadingly - termed piers.

Dating back to the first half of the 19th century, some pier lines were used as passenger lines from the outset (often as conversions of lines used by the contractors during the construction of the pier) whilst others began life as a suitable means of conveying passengers' baggage from ship to shore and back again; with the decline of the pleasure steamers a century later, however, such 'luggage lines' fell into disuse and disrepair unless they had already been converted to passenger-carrying.

A list of the different methods of propulsion used over the years on pier lines is about as varied as it could possibly be: hand, horse, steam, electric rail, battery, internal combustion, cable - and even, as befitting a close association with the sea - sail! Modifications were carried out and changes made on a sweeping scale made possible by the comparatively short lengths of track involved: electrification followed by de-electrification was almost the order of the day. Any attempt at standardisation of gauge, stock and the like was undreamt of: no probability existed of linking any two lines (although connections with other rail systems were occasionally envisaged and in one case - Ryde - actually made).

Sadly, the picture was to alter during the mid-20th century. The enforced pier closures and breachings of World War II, damage by sea and ships, a general drop in traffic levels and simple age-related structural deterioration all took their toll. Thankfully, in many cases the difficulties were overcome and the lines concerned have refused to die - though since the first edition of this book appeared a quarter of a century ago, two lines have closed. Ramsey possibly will re-open, Walton-on-the-Naze might (but only as another miniature railway) whilst the immediate prospects of Southport are a matter for concern. On the plus side, one totally new line - Blackpool North Pier - has joined their numbers.

Today, many of Britain's piers face a very uncertain future as the structural deterioration resulting from sheer old age reaches a critical stage. Although a number of vehicles from pier lines have been rescued for preservation or use elsewhere, no complete line has been saved in the same way that many of their grander, onshore cousins have been. With 1996 having been designated The Year of the Pier - a sign of the greater awareness and appreciation of the part played by the pier in Britain's transport and social history - perhaps it is only a matter of time before one is.

Another surviving line is that on Hythe pier. This postcard view shows one of its distinctive railway trains and the entry into the shore station loop. *Author's Collection*

The Blackpool North Pier tramway's three-car set at the shoreward end of Britain's newest pier line, outside the appropriately-named 'Tramstop Bar'.   *Author*

The set from the other side, looking towards the pier head.   *Author*

Chapter One

Blackpool North Pier Tramway

As befits its position as northern England's premier resort, the town of Blackpool boasts no less than three piers: North (opened in 1863), Central (1868) and South (1893), each catering for a different kind of clientele. Blackpool's newest tramway was constructed as part of a £6m refurbishment of the North Pier by its owner, the First Leisure Corporation, and was opened on Monday 2nd September, 1991, making it by far the youngest of the pier lines in the British Isles and a worthy addition to a town world-famous for its pioneering electric street tramway. The ½ mile-long pier has been much added to and damaged by ships, fire and storms over the years, one such incident occurring in the winter of 1990-91 when the fishermen's jetty at the pier head, and the sun lounge, were badly damaged by gales - hence the refurbishment.

The 3 ft gauge single-track line is laid with flat-bottomed rails, flush with the decking, on the (especially-strengthened) northern side of the mid-section of the pier and is partially roped-off from the rest of the promenade area. There are no passing loops or sidings. The tramway is worked by three similar, enclosed single-deck bogie cars coupled as a one-man-operated train and lettered BLACKPOOL NORTH PIER TRAMWAY. All three were custom-built by Harry Steer Engineering of Breaston, Derbyshire, with glass fibre colour-impregnated bodies mounted on galvanised steel chassis. The centre car houses a 2.3 litre Perkins diesel engine which, via a Linde variable-displacement hydraulic pump, drives wheel motors in the cars, the centre car having four of its eight wheels powered and the driving trailers two each of theirs similarly powered. Disc brakes are fitted. Another unconventional feature of the trams is that they have doors on their north (seaward) sides only. Livery is burgundy below the waistline and very pale cream above, with grey roofs, and the total train capacity 56 passengers (half seated and half standing).

Built to metric standards, the principal dimensions of the cars are:

Overall length:	5.4	m
Overall height:	2.7	m
Overall width:	1.5	m
Wheel diameter:	0.3	m
Power car weight:	5	tonnes
Trailer weight:	2	tonnes

Although comparatively short in length for a pier line, the 250 metre-long tramway is not simply a pleasure line but serves a useful purpose in ferrying passengers (at 75p return) between the landward and seaward structures on the pier in inclement weather - which the cars have been specially built to withstand, there being no shed facilities for them. Since 1998, all three Blackpool piers have been owned by Leisure Parcs Ltd.

[63 & 64 VICT.]   *Pier and Harbour Orders Confirmation (No. 2) Act,* 1900.   [63 & 64 VICT.]

[Ch. cxciii.]   *Pier and Harbour Orders Confirmation (No. 2) Act,* 1900.

A.D. 1900.
Felixstowe.

The SCHEDULE to which the foregoing Order refers.

I.—RATES FOR USE OF PIER.

	s.	d.
For every master or member of the crew of any vessel boat or wherry using the pier for the purpose of going to or returning from his own vessel boat or wherry an annual sum not exceeding	10	0
Or if the annual sum is not paid for each time	0	1
For every other person using the pier for the purpose of landing from or embarking on board of any ship vessel or boat of any kind whatever for each time any sum not exceeding	0	4
Save as above and save as herein-after mentioned for every person using the pier for each time any sum not exceeding	0	2
For every person using the pier between the hours of 6 p.m. and 10 p.m. on any day on which a concert or other public entertainment is held in any pavilion building or room for the time being on the pier for at least one and a half hours between the said hours of 6 p.m. and 10 p.m.	0	6
For every bath or sedan chair (including driver or carriers) taken on the pier for each time any sum not exceeding	0	4
For every perambulator (including driver) taken on the pier for each time any sum not exceeding	0	2

II.—RATES ON PASSENGERS' LUGGAGE LANDED SHIPPED OR TRANSHIPPED AT THE PIER.

For every trunk portmanteau box parcel or other package within the description of luggage and not borne by the passenger—

	s.	d.
Not exceeding 28 lbs. in weight	0	2
Over 28 lbs. and not exceeding 56 lbs.	0	3
Over 56 lbs. and not exceeding 84 lbs.	0	4
Over 84 lbs. and not exceeding 112 lbs.	0	5
Over 112 lbs. and not exceeding 140 lbs.	0	6
Over 140 lbs. and not exceeding 196 lbs.	0	7
Over 196 lbs. and not exceeding 2 cwts.	0	8
And for every 20 lbs. weight in addition or part thereof	0	1

III.—RATES ON GOODS SHIPPED TRANSHIPPED OR UNSHIPPED AT THE PIER.

	s.	d.
Ale beer and porter in cask per 54 gallons	0	6
Ale beer or porter bottled per 85 lbs.	0	4
Ael beer or porter bottled per dozen quarts	0	2
Ale beer or porter bottled per dozen pints	0	1
Anchors per cwt.	0	3
Anchor stock per foot run	0	3

26

FELIXSTOWE PIER.

Provisional Order for the Construction Maintenance and Regulation of a Pier and Works at Felixstowe in the County of Suffolk.

A.D. 1900.
Felixstowe.

Preliminary.

1. The Coast Development Company Limited shall be the undertakers for carrying this Order into execution. *[Undertakers.]*

In this Order unless the context otherwise requires— *[Interpretation.]*

The expression "the Company" means the Coast Development Company Limited.

The expression "the Council" means the Felixstowe and Walton Urban District Council.

The expression "the Conservancy Board" means the Harwich Harbour Conservancy Board.

Acquisition of Land.

2. The Lands Clauses Acts (except so much thereof as relates to the purchase and taking of lands otherwise than by agreement and to the entry upon lands by the promoters of the undertaking) are incorporated with this Order and for the purposes of that incorporation the term "special Act" in the said Acts shall mean this Order. *[Incorporation of Lands Clauses Acts.]*

3. For the purpose of the works authorised by this Order the Company may by agreement enter upon take and use such of the lands shown on the plan deposited for the purposes of this Order as they think requisite for the purpose of those works or any easement or right over or affecting those lands. *[Power to take lands.]*

4. Persons empowered by the Lands Clauses Acts to sell and convey or release lands may if they think fit subject to the provisions of those Acts and of this Order grant to the Company any easement right or privilege (not being an easement right or privilege of water in which persons other than the grantors have an interest) required for the purposes of this Order in over or affecting any such lands and the provisions of the said Acts with respect to lands and rent-charges so far as the same are applicable in this behalf shall extend and apply to such grants and to such easements rights and privileges as aforesaid respectively. *[Power to take easements by agreement.]*

5. This Order or anything contained therein shall not exempt the Company from any proceedings on account of any nuisance caused or permitted by them upon any land acquired by them under this Order. *[Nuisance not authorised.]*

Limits and Works.

6. The limits within which the Company shall have authority and which shall be deemed the limits to which this Order extends shall comprise the works authorised by this Order and the area below high-water mark lying within one hundred and fifty yards from any part of those works which is itself one hundred *[Limits.]*

25

Chapter Two

Felixstowe Pier Railway

Although Felixstowe has only really been developed as a major seaside resort during the last 60 years or so, the idea of adding a pier to the existing amenities was first promoted by the Coast Development Co. Ltd, a company formed in 1898 by a merger between Belle Steamers Ltd and various other local interests and already operating an electric pier railway further south at Walton-on-the-Naze (*see Chapter Nine*). It also owned a fleet of paddle steamers serving the East Coast.

Constructed under the Felixstowe Pier Order 1900, the pier was duly opened in August 1905 and stretched out to sea for a distance of ½ mile. Following the success of the one at Walton, a single-track electric railway (authorised by the 1900 Order) was laid during construction along the pier's north side from shore to pier head. Very similar in design to the Walton railway, it was laid to the same gauge of 3 ft 6 in. with 36 lb. running rails and had a centre rail fed with current from the local council's electricity works.

The rolling stock fleet consisted originally of one motor car and two trailers (builder unknown), each being an open-sided vehicle with cross-bench seating for 36 passengers beneath a flimsy-looking wooden roof. The lower bodywork was painted brown and the upper bodywork cream - possibly the same shade of maroon/mahogany brown as that used on the nearby Ipswich tramcars. Peckham trucks were fitted with that of the motor car being powered by a Thomas Parker motor. The three cars normally worked as one unit, though photographic evidence suggests that on occasion the motor car ran on its own (presumably when passengers were few). The fare of 3*d.* each way was collected by a conductor who issued tickets *en route* in tramway fashion.

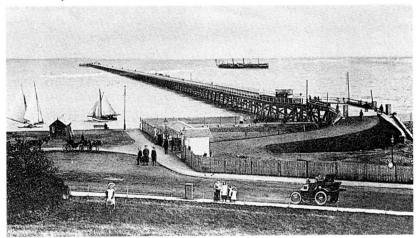

An early view of the pier with apparently only the one car in use on the railway.

G.F. Cordy Ltd

9

In the same year that the pier and railway opened, the Coast Development Co. Ltd was succeeded by the Coast Development Corporation Ltd, which concern went into liquidation in 1915 and was finally wound up seven years later. Both pier and railway were acquired by East Coast Piers Ltd who continued to keep the line running with its usual summer-only service.

Following the 1926 closure of the Ipswich Corporation Tramways, an old tramcar was purchased from there as a source of replacement components; this was No. 34 of the Ipswich fleet, built in 1904 by Brush as an open-top double-deck vehicle. Its body was mounted on a Brush AA truck powered by two 25 hp Westinghouse motors, the wheelbase was 6 ft and the gauge the same as that of the pier railway. The top deck fittings were removed prior to the car's delivery, and upon arrival at Felixstowe the remaining lower saloon was detached for use as a waiting-room at the pier head. In 1931 the body from the railway's original motor car was then mounted on the 'new' truck - which was even older than the 'old' truck - and this vehicle gave service until 1939 when the line closed. (During these years it in fact comprised the total stock of the railway, the other two cars having been scrapped in 1931.)

Inevitably, given the pier's East Coast location, the outbreak of World War II saw the suspension of services on Sunday 10th September, 1939, which turned into termination after the pier was irrevocably damaged by the sea. After the war the remnants at the seaward end were demolished completely, leaving just 450 ft of railway-less structure, rebuilt in concrete, the future development of which is currently a matter of debate.

Normal working on the line with all three 1905 cars running as one unit.   *G.F. Cordy Ltd*

Chapter Three

Herne Bay Pier Tramways

The plans for the first Herne Bay pier, designed by Thomas Rhodes under the supervision of Thomas Telford, show a double-track tramway running its length with a scissors crossover at the pier head; two branches are depicted as leading down to a lower level of the landing stage. As actually built, however, the tramway took the form of a single track from the shore to the pier head and its colossal, flag-waving statue of William IV; here also was sited the line's solitary, short siding and the whole arrangement was consequently far simpler than that originally proposed. The pier itself was constructed using 14 in. iron-clad timber piles and was justly famous from the outset as few other piers in Europe could match its 3,613 ft length. Its width was 24 ft (as opposed to the proposed 30 ft) and the structure was formally opened in June 1832 to serve steamers from London operated by the General Steam Navigation Co. In addition the owner of the pier, the Herne Bay Pier Co., was responsible for the construction of a 50 ft-wide, mile-long parade along the seafront.

It seems likely that the tramway was laid at the time of the pier's construction (although not mentioned in the pier's 1831 authorising Act), thus making it the first pier line in Great Britain - and probably the first such line in the world. Hand-propelled 4-wheeled wagons were used on the narrow gauge line for the conveyance of the steamer passengers' luggage, thus establishing the historical precedent for the other pier lines that followed during the 19th century. The line was certainly in working order by Thursday 13th June, 1833 for on that date the tramway's sail-powered car made its maiden run. This vehicle bore the proud title of *Old Neptune's Car* and was the brainchild of the local landowner and pier financier, Sir Henry-Chudleigh Oxenden, a man of many years' experience with ice and land yachts. Fitted with a lug sail for when the wind was favourable (and hand-propelled by two or three porters when it was not), the car apparently also carried passengers as well as their luggage.

The use of sail power was not without its hazards, as at least one fatality is on record as having been caused by the car's swift and silent progress - on Tuesday 2nd June, 1840 when a woman with a wooden leg (one Jane Harris) was run over by the Pier Master - as well as several other serious accidents. There was, however, a more light-hearted side to the picture, as portrayed by the then editor of *Punch*, Douglas Jenold, in his magazine of 1842 (Vol. III, No. 55):

> The approach to Herne Bay is by a wooden pier nearly twice the extent of the town, as the tide in these parts runs sometimes as low as the rents. This landing-place is strongly defended by two ship guns and six wheelbarrows. The garrison at present consists of four ticket-porters, who are exercised three or four times a day, under the command of a glazed cap and a gold-laced band, in propelling a machine very like a diligence [a French public stage-coach] in reduced circumstances, in which the steamboat passengers and luggage are conveyed at the rate of two-pence a head and two-pence a *trunk*.

Jenold was a frequent visitor to Herne Bay, which by this date was well on its way to becoming a respectable Victorian watering-hole. In 1831, for example, the population of this little North Kent village had reached 1,876 after a long and gradual climb, only to shoot up to 3,041 over the next decade. During these years, as well as promoting and building the pier, local business interests had been intent upon developing a seven-mile strip of coast independent of the old village of Herne just inland.

By the late 1840s Jenold's mood had changed for the 'garrison' had committed the cardinal error of crushing Mrs Jenold's brand new Parisian bonnet-box - complete with brand new Parisian bonnet - and had then demanded porterage! From then on Jenold scathingly ridiculed Herne Bay in the pages of his magazine with such squibs as this one from an 1849 (Vol. XVII) issue:

> Our latest dates from this locality go back as far as the end of June, which may be accounted for by the blockade of high steamboat fares being still continued. The pier proprietors co-operate cordially in the blockade, and aid, by prohibition pier dues, the prohibition prices of the steamboats, while the prohibition fares of the South Eastern Railway do their part in the establishment of the somewhat contradictory policy of keeping the public literally at Bay, by keeping everybody away from it.

Little is known about the following period of the tramway's life and exactly how many other cars were eventually used is uncertain. In 1848 Jenold still referred to only one sail-car, though this was a flat-bed vehicle and not the enclosed 'diligence' referred to above whose passengers could ride on the roof as well as inside. What is certain is that the whole development of the resort turned sour. The village stopped growing so that in 1861, the same year that saw it put on the railway map with the arrival of the Margate Railway from its junction with the London, Chatham & Dover Railway at Faversham, the population stood at only 3,147 with worse to come: the closing of the 1862 summer season was followed in October by the termination of the steamer service from London. To cap it all, the effects of harsh winter storms and the ravages of the toredo worm were being felt by the wooden pier and closure was deemed necessary in view of the unsound condition of the 30-year-old structure. The closure was finally effected in 1864 and seven years later the remains were sold for scrap with plans being made for a completely new, iron structure to be sited 80 yards to the east.

Work on this second project was carried out under the Herne Bay Promenade Pier Order 1872 by the newly-formed Herne Bay Pavilion, Promenade & Pier Co. Ltd and completed in 1873; the opening ceremony was performed in the August of that year by Sir Sidney Waterloo, Lord Mayor of London. As opened, the pier at 320 ft was only a tenth of the length of the one it replaced but, under the Herne Bay Pier Order 1891, permission was given to the owner (now retitled as the Herne Bay Pier Co. Ltd) to widen and considerably extend it. Powers were also included in this Order for the laying of a tramway or tramways for the carriage of all classes of goods, to be worked by any form of motive power. In 1896 work began on the extension and a track laid down the centre for a crane to run on; in view of the envisaged length of the pier the intention was to use this as the basis of a passenger tramway and a further Herne Bay Pier Order, in 1896, gave permission for this on condition that the line was inspected and certified by the Board of Trade. Opened in June 1898, with an official opening not until 14th September, 1899, the finished structure was, at 3,787 ft, then the second longest pier in England (after Southend-on-Sea).

The tramway was worked using electric traction, adopted by the simple expedient of utilising the existing crane rails with the addition of an off-centre conduit installed by the British Thomson-Houston Co. Ltd of Rugby. This was formed from 2 in. x 2 in. steel angle and carried a conductor fed with current at 250v DC from the pier's own generator. The gauge of the track has been given variously as 3 ft or 3 ft 6 in but A.W. Bond, writing in *Modern Tramway* of April 1968, states that he measured it as 3 ft 4½ in. - a gauge probably casually referred to at the time as simply 'three feet' or 'three and a half feet', thus giving rise to the confusion. The running rails rested on 14 in. longitudinal sleepers laid over the main girders of the pier and cross-bonded at 40 yard intervals. At the end of 1898 two Peckham Cantilever reversed maximum traction trucks, each powered by a General Electric 60 25 hp motor, were delivered to the line, shortly followed by an enclosed single-deck car body from Brush. After assembly, the first trial outing of the car took place in January 1899; Major Cardew of the Board of Trade formally inspected the line on 17th March that year and passed it fit for passenger traffic.

The tramway opened to the public on Saturday 1st April and consisted of a single straight track running unfenced from a marquee a hundred yards or so out from the shore (where the pier had been widened to accommodate a proposed Grand Pavilion) to the restaurant at the pier head, terminating at a buffer stop just in front of the door. A shore-end pavilion (erected in 1883) housed a 50 kW GE generator, driven by a gas engine, which also supplied current for the pier's lights. The sole passenger vehicle on the line was the Brush car, numbered 1, which seated 28 on cross benches and weighed just under 7 tons. Presumably this proved unable to cope with traffic demands on its own for it was joined in May 1901 by two standard gauge vehicles purchased from the Bristol Tramways & Carriage Co. Ltd, owner of the Bristol horse tramways, and sold to the Herne Bay line as surplus to requirements following the electrification of the system. These were Bristol Nos. 47 and 47, both 4-wheeled roofed toastracks with seating for 30 passengers and probably dating from the late 1870s. Each weighed 1 ton 12 cwt. They were given the new numbers 2 and 3 and, after regauging, were attached as driving trailers to each end of the motor car (with No. 3 to seaward). Communication bells were fitted, operated by the driver's foot and by the conductor via a sliding rod. The line's fourth vehicle was a 4-wheeled luggage trolley built by Dick, Kerr & Co. Ltd of Preston which was pushed down the pier by the rest of the rake to serve the steamers now once again making the journey out from London.

On Tuesday 16th July, 1901 the tramway's most serious accident occurred. The luggage trolley, being propelled in the normal manner, suddenly left the track and jammed against the railings on one side of the pier. The driver panicked and leapt from the leading trailer, along with the conductor and two of the passengers. No-one apparently had even thought of applying the brakes and the driving trailer was pushed through the railings, broke its coupling and plummeted into the sea. One elderly lady passenger, Sarah Pearce of Brixton, was killed instantly and all services were suspended immediately. At the subsequent inquest the jury

Work underway on the extension of the second Herne Bay pier (1896-98); the off-centre conduit laid in the crane track can be clearly seen.   *Courtesy Herne Bay Records Society*

Conduit working: a rake of cars about to depart from the pier head.

Courtesy Herne Bay Records Society

recommended that the practice of pushing the trolley in front of the train should cease whilst the coroner stated that he had decided not to inform the Board of Trade (!) of the accident and that no blame was attached to anyone (!!).

After the necessary repairs had been carried out the line re-opened, but it soon became apparent that the tramway was running at a loss and matters finally came to a head in 1905 when the General Manager, Mr H.C. Jones, was successfully prosecuted for embezzlement. The pier passed into the hands of the debenture holders and on 17th February that year a Mr F.W. Wacher was appointed Receiver. On 5th November Wacher reached an agreement with Herne Bay Urban District Council to take over the pier, the sale being sanctioned by the Herne Bay Pier Act of that year. The actual transfer took place on 30th September, 1909 (under the Herne Bay Pier Order 1909), the UDC paying the sum of £6,000 for the pier and tramway. Apart from the revenue obtained from ships, pedestrians and passengers, a total of £227 10s. was received yearly from the various sweet sellers, chemists and tobacconists, etc. who had premises on the pier. In addition, a rental of £90 per year was obtained from the Automatic Sweetmeat Co. who operated several vending machines there.

The new owner continued to run the pier and tramway in the same manner as before (though it finally managed to open the Grand Pier Pavilion in 1910). Sample tolls and fares, fixed since the opening of the pier, were as follows:

Passengers embarking or disembarking	4*d*.	
Using the pier for pleasure	2*d*.	
Bath or 'sedan' chairs (with occupant)	4*d*.	
Tramway passengers	3*d*.	
Light goods conveyed per cubic foot	1*d*.	
Heavy goods per ton	2*s*.	
Passengers' trunks, cases etc.	2*d*.	upwards

With the outbreak of World War I the steamer trade once again ceased and the tramway closed. The cars became temporary shelters on the army-guarded pier (with the motor car body, removed from its trucks, resting on timber baulks) and were later sold for scrap, so ending the second period of the tramway's turbulent life. (A correspondent, Mr M.C. Moore of Croydon, recounts that during their annual summer holidays at this time, he and his brother would take great delight in freeing a trailer's hand-brake wheel and annoying everyone in the vicinity with the noise they could make with the pawl and rachet!)

The inter-war years saw out the whole of the line's third and final era. After World War I the steamers returned and the Council decided to re-equip the tramway and, after some deliberation, a petrol-electric tramcar was ordered from the local firm of Strode Engineering. Duly delivered in July 1925, it began active service on August Bank Holiday that year. In design the brown and cream car was both unusual and unreliable and regarded as something of a joke by its passengers. The centrally-positioned petrol engine was coupled to the dynamo via a chain and the water cooling tank was on the roof; the chain frequently broke and the water just as frequently boiled. Together with a substantial increase in traffic its shortcomings meant that a new car was needed desperately if the line was to be run at a profit. The old conduit having been

The conduit tramway, looking back from the pier head, as depicted on an early souvenir postcard, posted 1906 in London.   *Author's Collection*

Aftermath of the accident of 16th July, 1901: the fallen trailer being salvaged. The vehicle top right is the original Brush motor car.   *Courtesy Herne Bay Records Society*

The Herne Bay pier tramway as depicted on the 1908 edition Ordnance Survey 6 in. map.

[**Ch. cxv.**] *Pier and Harbour Orders Confirmation* [9 EDW. 7.]
                  (*No. 2*) *Act*, 1909.

		£	s.	d.

A.D. 1909.

Herne Bay.

V.—RATES FOR USE OF WEIGHING MACHINES.

For goods weighed for each ton or part of a ton   -   - 0 0 2

VI.—RATES FOR USE OF TRAMWAY.

For every passenger using tramway for each time any sum not
   exceeding   -   -   -   -   -   -   - 0 0 3
Light goods per cubic foot   -   -   -   -   - 0 0 1
Heavy goods per ton   -   -   -   -   -   - 0 2 0
   For passengers' luggage rates not exceeding rates on same
   for use of pier.

Rates for the use of the tramway as laid down in the Schedule to the 1909 Herne Bay Pier Order.

Edwardian postcard of the pier head, complete with tramway buffer stop. The off-centre
conduit is clearly visible.   *Author's Collection*

Another Edwardian postcard view of the pier, this time showing the shore entrance and, in the middle distance, the original marquee 'pavilion' with solitary car No. 1 just visible beyond it - suggesting that the original photograph might date to the very earliest days of the line.

Author's Collection

The same view, shortly after the Grand Pier Pavilion opened in 1910; it was destroyed by fire 60 years later. The horse still ruled the road - as also evidenced by the continuing presence of the horse trough on the right. *Author's Collection*

removed (presumably for scrap during the war), various other forms of propulsion were considered. Finally F.C. Hibberd & Co. Ltd of London were contracted to supply a battery-powered car capable of seating 48 passengers. Driven by an 11 hp Metrovick motor, the closed vehicle was delivered from Hibberd's Park Royal Coachworks and entered service in 1934 with the Strode car adapted to serve as a trailer. The batteries for the Hibberd car were charged in a corrugated-iron shed at the shore end of the line; built over the single line (which still had no sidings) the shed was the closest the tramway ever came to providing any sort of depot for its stock. Its livery has been given variously as both brown and cream and green and cream.

By 1939 traffic was sufficiently heavy to warrant a regular service every 15 minutes from 9.30 am to 6.00 pm. The service was, however, doomed for the outbreak of World War II saw the suspension of the steamer services yet again and the closure of the pier to the public. Like its counterpart across the Thames at Southend, the pier was heavily fortified. On Friday 3rd November that year the last tram ran back to the shore and the pier was later breached in two places for defence purposes. History repeated itself for what survived of the cars was sold as scrap after the war, fetching the princely sum of £12 10s. The pier was later repaired (though the greater portion of it was closed as unsafe in 1968 and partially destroyed in a gale ten years later, leaving the pier head isolated) but the tramway remained just a memory.

Under the auspices of the Urban District Council: the Hibberd battery car and trailer at the pier head terminus (now equipped with low platforms and enlarged canopy). The conduit has been removed.   *Courtesy Herne Bay Records Society*

Chapter Four

Hythe Pier Tramway and Railway

The pier at Hythe in Hampshire was constructed, at a cost of £7,700 by Messrs Bergheim & Co. of London, under the Hythe Pier Order 1878 (after two earlier promotions had come to nothing) by the Hythe Pier & Hythe & Southampton Ferry Co. Ltd and was officially opened on the first day of 1881 (a Saturday) by the Mayor of Southampton. Its purpose was to develop the existing steamer ferry service across the broad mouth of the River Test to Southampton Town Quay (this being the latest in a centuries-old series of ferry services at this location). In order to provide a continuous service the pier was built, of iron, to a length of 2,100 ft so as to reach deep water even at low tide with passengers' luggage being transported by means of handcarts. These however were found to damage the decking - which had to be replaced completely in 1896 - and consequently, in view of the number of passengers using the pier (124,533 in the first year), it was decided in February 1909 to lay a tramway (authorised by the 1878 Order) along it. Constructed that spring and early summer by a local undertaker, E.J. Kingham, and opened by the end of July, this ran off-centre down the north side of the 16 ft-wide pier and was worked with two open-sided 4-wheeled trucks which were hand-propelled in normal luggage line fashion. (Plans for an earlier pier show a tramway envisaged as well.) It was laid flush with the decking as a very narrow gauge single track to which was added, the following February, a number of short sidings. The original line and/or at least some of the sidings appear to have extended out onto the roadway at the shore end of the pier. Further trucks were then acquired to cope with traffic demands.

After World War I the owners decided to adapt the line for passenger traffic using the third-rail electric system. As rebuilt, the railway was laid with 20 lb. flat-bottomed rails to a gauge of 2 ft - the narrowness of this gauge suggests that it was that of the old tramway, possibly even with the existing rails being re-used - on a new location close to the south side of the pier. The third rail was laid on the seaward side of the line, as appears to have been standard pier railway practice for added safety. This was fed with a supply of current at 100v DC taken from the local generating station (stepped down from 200v at the pier). With the village's change to AC mains, the power was from then on taken from the national grid, via a rectifier. The actual track layout has not been altered since it was laid and consists of a single track from the pier head station to the shore where there is a short siding parallel to the main line and a short, second siding which curves off sharply from the first to run into the coach shed. Neither of these sidings is electrified and stock using them has therefore to be propelled by hand - an interesting throwback to the original tramway! The line along the pier is, of course, fenced-off from the rest of the decking.

The choice of motive power was somewhat unusual: three tiny Brush battery locomotives were purchased second-hand from the Ministry of Munitions' Avonmouth Mustard Gas Works and the batteries removed from their ledges fore and aft of the central cabs. Built in 1917, they originally operated on 100v

An early postcard view of a Hythe pier train at the shore station, probably just after the line opened, showing two driving trailers, one ordinary trailer, a locomotive and a luggage truck, and a non-plussed (or should that be four-plussed?) gentleman and cloche-hatted companion - and an impatient driver?   *Author's Collection*

A post-World War II postcard view of the pier with trailer, tank wagon and flat wagon just visible to the right.   *Author's Collection*

4726.   HYTHE PIER FROM DRUMMOND HOTEL.

Exide 'Ironclad' batteries. Works Nos. 16302 (No. 1) and 16307 (No. 2) were fitted with collector shoes at Hythe whilst the third locomotive was dismantled to provide a comprehensive range of spares for the other two. The original 5½ hp motors still run quite happily, driving each locomotive's four 16 in. wheels via a chain transmission. Overall dimensions of the locomotives are: length 8 ft 4 in., height 6 ft 9 in., width 3 ft 9 in. The wheels are set at 3 ft centres. The locomotives entered service upon the railway's opening in 1922 and are capable of hauling 6 tons at 12 mph.

Passenger rolling stock was supplied as new in 1921 by the Drewry Car Co. Ltd, there being two bogie driving trailers (length 16 ft 2 in., height 7 ft 1 in., width 5 ft) and two bogie ordinary trailers (16 ft by 7 ft 6 in. by 5 ft) which, when running, are totally out of proportion to the diminutive locomotives. Wheel diameter is 14 in. A driving compartment is fitted with duplicate controls at the seaward end of each driving trailer and is used on the outward journey to the pier head. Once premises of the Royal Motor Yacht Club were sited here, but since World War II the buildings have been converted into a restaurant and buffet room. Each driving trailer seats 16-18 in two compartments while the ordinary trailers seat 18-20 in three compartments.

Goods stock is made up of two 4-wheeled luggage trucks 7 ft long by 3 ft 6 in. wide and fitted with 'double decks' some 18 in. apart, and one 4-wheeled tank truck, 7 ft 6 in. long by 3 ft 6 in. wide. The wooden frame of this truck supports a large steel tank which is used for supplying the ferry boats with fuel oil. Both passenger and goods vehicles are fitted with centre buffers above the couplings, though the tank-truck lacks one coupling as it is always placed at the seaward end of a train when in use, and since the line lacks a turntable is never turned. Locomotives and coaches alike were formerly painted a uniform shade of green, later changed to green with cream window frames with the initials 'H P R' emblazoned on the doors, but in 1963 upper and lower bodywork was repainted a light shade of royal blue and white respectively, changing in 1996 to red and white. (Immediately prior to this last change the trailers were lettered 'Waterfront Line'.) The coaches are fitted with internal lighting via a cable connection to the locomotive.

The line is worked by one locomotive at a time together with a usual train of the two ordinary trailers plus a driving trailer at the seaward end (plus a goods vehicle if needed); photographic evidence from the railway's early years however would seem to suggest that most of the stock was originally operated together as one train with an engine at each end. The driver acts as conductor before the trains starts and collects the tickets for the outward trip; he also sells tickets for the return journey to the shore. The fare was originally 1*d*. each way - raised inevitably over the years - and the service is run to connect with the steamers which call, normally every half-hour. In 1973 it was announced that only ferry passengers would be permitted to use the train in an attempt to resolve the problem of overcrowding during the high season but this decision met with much local opposition on behalf of those residents and holidaymakers who used the pier for recreation. The problem was resolved by allowing the train drivers some discretion in the matter, especially regarding elderly patrons of the pier.

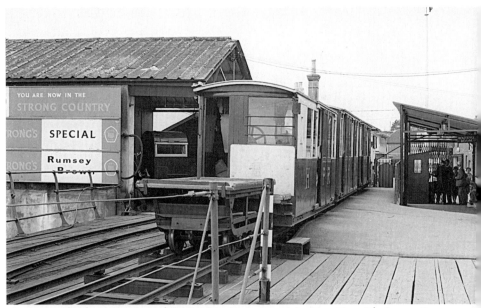

Stock at the shore station on 4th July, 1964, a luggage truck leading. One of the locomotives can be seen in the coach shed at the end of the non-electrified siding.   *T.J. Edgington*

One of the diminutive Brush locomotives with a train of two trailers and one control trailer, in green and cream livery, in mid-journey.   *J.H. Meredith, courtesy Lens of Sutton*

The pier head station with a train ready to depart on 26th September, 1970. *T.J. Edgington*

Nineteen years on, a similar train waits to depart from the pier head on 19th October, 1989.
J.H. Meredith, courtesy Lens of Sutton

Another view of the pier head station, again on 19th October, 1989.
J.H. Meredith, courtesy Lens of Sutton

The Hythe pier train as usually operated today: one locomotive, two ordinary trailers and a driving trailer, as captured by the camera on 8th April, 1995.   *P.G. Barnes*

In 1923 the owning company shortened its rather verbose title to the Hythe Pier Co. Ltd and still retains ownership of the pier, while the ferry service was taken over by the General Estates Co. Ltd, the majority shareholders in the HP Co., and who also operated the railway on lease from the HP Co., under the provision of the 1878 Order. Little has changed on the line since its opening though the entrance to the pier was modernised during the early 1960s and the pier head similarly treated in 1970-71; in 1992 ownership of ferries and tramway passed to the newly-incorporated Kent concern, White Horse Ferries Ltd. Probably the line's proudest moment was when during World War II, just before D-Day, King George VI crossed over from Southampton and rode the line in a specially cleaned and guarded train.

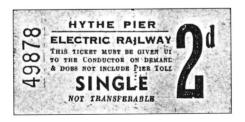

A postcard view of the Queen's Pier, Ramsey during the inter-war years, alas with no tram in sight.
Author's Collection

The tiny 1937 'Planet' locomotive and trailer at the pier head.
W.C. Ellis

Chapter Five

Ramsey Queen's Pier Tramway

The Isle of Man has long - and deservedly - been famous for the astonishing diversity of its railways and tramways, and it comes as little surprise to find a pier line numbered among them. Unfortunately, like the Groudle Glen Railway, it has always tended to be overshadowed by the more immediately noticeable and picturesque lines but, unlike that railway, has not been resurrected after closure yet.

Its history began on Thursday 22nd July, 1886 when Queen's Pier, Ramsey, was formally opened by the Lord Bishop of Sodor and Man. The 2,160 ft-long iron pier was built by Messrs Head, Wrightson & Son of Stockton-on-Tees and it is believed that they incorporated the tramway into the structure during construction, using it for the transport of materials and equipment. The pier was intended to serve the Manx pleasure steamers, the Douglas ferries to Belfast and Ardrossan and the Ramsey service to Whitehaven, the tramway being used for the conveyance of passengers' baggage after its opening.

In the usual manner of such luggage lines the tramway ran down the centre of the pier not in any way fenced-off from the decking on either side. The lay-out was that of a single track with a central passing loop, a short siding at the pier head, another close to the shore and two short, diverging spurs on to the road at the pier entrance. These two spurs were removed 1955-56 and replaced by a short, straight section laid with ex-Douglas horse tramway rails. Total length of the line was 2,080 ft. The gauge adopted was the Isle of Man standard of 3 ft and the track laid with 45 lb. tramway-type grooved rails which (apart from certain point sections) were never replaced during the lifetime of the line.

The original fleet of rolling stock was made up of seven 4-wheeled trucks of two basic designs and one 4-wheeled flat wagon. Propulsion was by hand and the line had the distinction of being the first - and only - pier tramway on the island. A new landing stage was opened at the pier head in 1899 (bringing the pier's total length to 2,241 ft) and in August that year a passenger vehicle entered service. This closed van boasted the luxury of upholstered seats (for some half-dozen passengers at a squeeze) and was also propelled by hand. At the same time a vague proposal was put forward for linking the line with the rest of the town (a little to the north) as an electric tramway; the idea was revived in 1906 when the same-gauge Manx Electric Railway (MER), which had reached Ramsey from Laxey in 1899, showed interest in the scheme but once again the plan was let drop.

The line clung to the outmoded system of manual working until as late a date as 1937 when the tramway was finally modernised. That May the Isle of Man Harbour Board (the owner of both pier and tramway) purchased a tiny petrol locomotive and trailer from F.C. Hibberd & Co. Ltd of London. The 'Planet' class locomotive, Works No. 2027, was powered by an 8 hp engine and the bogie trailer, roofed toast-rack Works No. 2028, seated 10 in comfort and 15 at a pinch on its five seats. The old passenger van was retired to serve as a stationary store but four of the luggage trucks were retained to perform their original duties. In August 1950

Hibberd 'Planet' locomotive 2027 and shuttered trailer 2028 parked in the shore siding on 23rd June, 1963.   *T.J. Edgington*

Wickham railcar 5763 by the pier entrance on the same day. Note the tramcar-style reversible seats.   *T.J. Edgington*

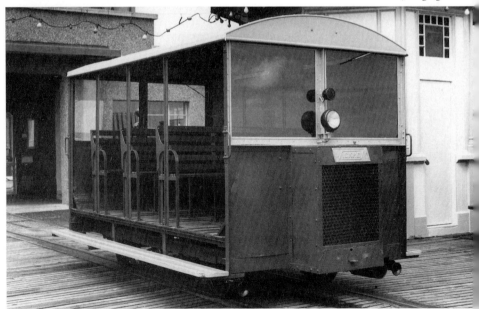

The 'Planet' locomotive and trailer in operation at the pier head, 4th July, 1965.   *T.J. Edgington*

The 'Planet' locomotive and trailer at the shore terminus, 1975; note the trailer's shutters down on the north side as protection against the wind.   *Author*

The shore end siding, 1975, with a large luggage truck nearest the camera and a smaller version beyond.   *Author*

The desolate pier in 1993 with one large and two small luggage trucks stacked together on the shore end siding.   *Author*

one further addition was made to the stock: a new Wickham railcar (Works No. 5763, Pattern No. 27) powered by a Ford V8 petrol engine and fitted with side shutters and toastrack seating for 10 (or 12 at another pinch). The livery of the stock is thought to have always been red (with the 'Planet' locomotive green until *c*. 1960).

As elsewhere in the British Isles, the coastal steamer trade shrank markedly after World War II and at Ramsey the number of steamer pasengers using the pier dropped from more than 36,000 a year before 1914 to just 3,054 in 1969; at the close of the 1969 summer season Tynwald (the Isle of Man Parliament) approved the intention of the Harbour Board to close the pier to steamers on condition that it - and the tramway - remained open to anglers and holidaymakers for as long as possible. In the event this meant the end of steamer use in September 1970 with the pier remaining open until the end of the 1981 season when it was discovered that extensive (and expensive) replacement of the wooden track bearers was needed. So, on Wednesday 9th September, 1981, the tramway was closed by the Manx Electric Railway Society, its operator during its final years, having carried some 7,000 passengers over 900 car miles during its last season of operations.

The 'Planet' locomotive and trailer were given by the Harbour Board to the Ramsey Commissioners who were considering constructing a pleasure line in the town's Mooragh Park, but this idea came to nothing and they are now owned by the Isle of Man Railway & Tramway Preservation Society and stored at Ramsey and operated on the MER there on special occasions such as during the 1993 Year of the Railways celebrations, the locomotive sporting an extremely unconvincing dummy boiler and chimney. The Wickham railcar was acquired earlier by the Isle of Man Railway and used (with the 'Planet' locomotive) in the dismantling of its St Johns-Ramsey line in 1975; after the completion of this task its engine was found to be life-expired and the car was broken up, presumably as a source of spare parts for the railway's small fleet of similar works vehicles.

That was the situation for more than a decade but, following the spectacular success of the 1993 railway celebrations (especially in terms of the dramatic increase in the number of visitors to the island), the Government decided that the pier was too valuable an asset to lose and the sum of £40,000 per year was allocated for its maintenance and gradual restoration. The bulk of the tramway remains intact and, at present, it is well within the bounds of possibility that it will one day operate again. A glimpse of what might be was provided on Sunday 30th June, 1996 when the first third of the pier was re-opened for National Piers Day, the occasion celebrated with festivities organised by the Friends of Ramsey Pier group and the 'Planet' locomotive on display in its old home.

The only other pier on the island was at Douglas. Opened in 1869, it was dismantled 1895-96 and re-erected at Rhos-on-Sea in North Wales where it stood until its 1954 demolition. At neither site is it thought to have carried a line.

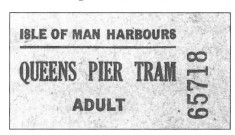

Looking through the locked entrance gates at Ramsey, 1993, with the stub track out to the roadway now obliterated.   *Author*

The 'Planet' locomotive (now with a rather unconvincing 'steam' outline) and trailer in the rain at the Ramsey terminus of the Manx Electric Railway, taking part in the 1993 'Year of the Railways' celebrations.   *Author*

Chapter Six

Ryde Pier Tramway and Railway

The first Ryde pier was opened as long ago as 1814, the Ryde Pier Co. having been formed just two years earlier under an 1812 Act. Of wooden construction, it stretched for 1,704 ft over the mudflats of the foreshore to the deep waters of the Solent, and was intended for use in conjunction with the Southsea-Ryde ferry service and so cash in on the Isle of Wight's growing popularity as a holiday resort. It was lengthened in stages to 2,250 ft and, in 1825, the ferry sailing ships were replaced by steamers. However, the pier was regarded as being too long a walk by luggage-laden passengers and little traffic was attracted away from the rival Southampton-Cowes service.

It was not until 1857 that the Ryde Pier Co. considered laying a tramway down the pier; even then nothing was done until two years later when its hand was forced by the sanctioning of the Cowes-Newport railway which would greatly increase Cowes' importance. The following year saw the passing of the Act for the Ryde-Ventnor line and, on 31st March, 1861, the company resolved to lay a tramway to help capture as great a part as possible of the growing holiday traffic. Constructed by a local contractor, John Langdon, the horse-drawn tramway finally opened for passenger traffic on Monday 29th August, 1864 (though it is thought that a hand-propelled luggage service had been operated since the previous autumn). The opening had in fact been delayed for several months after completion of the work in order to carry out locomotive trials. The original intention had been to use a steam locomotive on the line and, in accordance with this policy, in November 1863 the Leeds firm of Manning, Wardle & Co. Ltd was requested to supply 'a small locomotive engine, 6 in. cylinder and 12 in. stroke, in working trim, 6½ tons, sufficient to move a gross load of 96 tons on the level'. (The probable reason for such a powerful specification will become clear later.) It was requested for a trial period of three months and duly arrived on 14th March, 1864, complete with Mr Wardle himself to operate it.

The first trial took place on the same day it arrived, earning the locomotive the distinction of being the first steam engine to work a pier line - in fact, Ryde was the only pier line that saw steam working. The locomotive, named *Vectis* from the Latin name for the island, was a class 'B' 0-4-0 saddle tank (Works No. 111) with an ordinary horizontal boiler and 2 ft 6 in. diameter wheels but with the whole machine enclosed in a cab. The exhaust steam was condensed by admission to the water tank, and it appears to have been the first independent tramway locomotive ever built. Only two trials actually took place along the standard gauge line from the pier head to the shore, for by 19th March the company Directors were alarmed at the amount of vibration it set up in their pier and halted the tests. The locomotive was subsequently returned to the makers in May (and later sold to the North Fleet Coal Co. in Kent), the sum of £152 having been the cost of its hire.

A passenger car was then commissioned from a Mr T.B. Ayshford of Britannia Works, Walham Green, London, that June. It arrived damaged by the

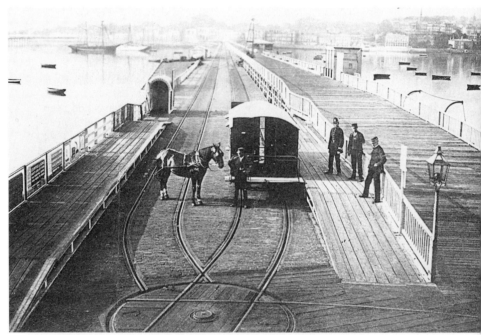

Ryde pier head in very early days before the 1871 extension of the tramway to St John's Road was opened. The turntable allowed the solitary passenger car to be turned and provided access to the car shed.   *Lens of Sutton*

View of the pier head *c.* 1875 showing the two separate ticket huts for the Esplanade and St John's Road. The rear car on the left is the 'Grapes' car in original double-deck form. Other cars are stored to the left of the running lines just beyond the new crossover.   *Lens of Sutton*

Solent crossing but after hasty repairs had been made public services, at long last, began. Costing £220, it had a first class compartment seating 16 and a second class one for 20 with space for a further 12 on the end driving platforms. Length was 22 ft, width 8 ft, height 6 ft and weight 1 ton 15 cwt. (It has been suggested that this vehicle was an adapted horse omnibus and, at such an early date in British tramway history, this is more than likely.) The 1st class fare was 4*d*. a trip, 2nd class was 2*d*.

It soon became apparent that the tramway was not as effective as had been envisaged as passengers for parts of the island other than Ryde were still faced with a long walk from the Esplanade (at the shore end of the pier) to the Isle of Wight (Eastern Section) Railway's (IWR) station in St John's Road on the other side of the town. It was decided therefore to extend the tramway to the station - a move strongly opposed by the Ryde Town Commissioners and not completed until the Ryde Pier and Tramways Act 1865, the Ryde Pier Railway Act 1867 and the Ryde Pier Railway Extension Act 1870 had all been obtained. (In view of the specification for *Vectis*, it would seem that through working from the railway station was secretly planned for from the beginning.) The first section to Ryde Castle (1,180 ft) ran south-east from the pier toll gate along a widened Esplanade and opened on Friday 28th January, 1870; the remaining portion (bringing the total length of the line to 1½ miles) opened to traffic on Saturday 7th August, 1871 and ran south from here through (literally!) Holywell House into Cornwall Street then beside the culverted Monkton Road Brook, across Link Road and Park Road to an end-on connection with the railway at the station. A short section of the tramway here was used by the railway's engines to run round their trains.

The physical linkage of the railway and the (principally single-track) tramway meant that IWR goods vans could be hauled to the pier head. In 1873 a further extension was completed. This branch of the tramway, at the other end of the Esplanade from the pier, ran back parallel to the passenger line on reclaimed land to the harbour basins at the shore end of Victoria Pier; this was used for goods traffic only. Built in 1864 to a length of 700 ft, Victoria Pier replaced an earlier structure but succumbed to the ravages of the sea in the early 1920s.

Its full line in place, the company once again decided to investigate the advantages - and disadvantages - of steam traction and in 1876 hired a tram engine from Merryweather & Sons of London for further trials. These began on 29th September (after a short trial on the Landport & Southsea Tramways across the Solent in Portsmouth) along the pier only as local opposition prevented road running. The Mayor and Corporation were present at the first trial and apparently were impressed with the engine's performance, though the Board of Trade ruled its use on the pier section illegal; at the end of the year the engine - one of Merryweather's 'standard' enclosed tram engines - was consequently returned to the makers, and the horses continued to plod.

Although the extension to St John's Road had improved matters somewhat, the transfers between steamer and tram, and tram and train, did little to attract passengers to the Southsea-Ryde route; consequently in 1877 the London & South Western Railway and the London, Brighton & South Coast Railway jointly obtained authority for a new pier and rail link to St John's Road. The section from the latter station to the Esplanade was opened on 5th April, 1880, and the line on the new railway pier (on the eastern side of the old, promenade pier) on 12th July of the same year. The line ran under the streets of the town in a tunnel from Monkton Street almost to the end of the pier where an intermediate station (Ryde Esplanade) was sited on the sharp curve between the horse tramway and the sea, and from there along the new pier.

The railway line was used jointly by the IWR and the Isle of Wight Central Railway; the joint owners of the new pier had no stock on the island at all. The same year that saw the opening of the railway pier also saw the demise of the tram in the streets of Ryde, and the 10*d*. (1st class) and 5*d*. (2nd class) fares from the Pier Head to St John's Road became things of the past with the trams working the track on the pier only, the extension metals being lifted that April.

The actual layout of the pier tramway consisted of a double track down the eastern side of the pier, not separated in any way from the rest of the decking. At either end the lines converged (with the inner rails actually crossing) to feed a wooden turntable which provided the necessary means of turning the horse cars after each journey. The turntable at the Pier Head station fed a short siding and carriage shed across the end of the pier, whilst that at the Pier Toll Gate station formerly made another right-angle 'point' with the line along the Esplanade to St John's Road. Simple crossovers were also fitted at each end, but these were later removed.

At the time of opening rolling stock had consisted of just two vehicles: the Ayshford car and a small luggage van. By 1880 the fleet had grown to six open-top double-deck cars, two closed single-deck cars and a variety of luggage vans and trucks which were horse-hauled behind scheduled passenger cars. (In 1870, in one of the company's few official returns, 19 goods vehicles were listed.) Some of the passenger cars were almost certainly supplied by a leading manufacturer of the period, the Starbuck Car & Wagon Co. Ltd of Birkenhead, but precise details are tantalizingly lacking. Livery is thought to have been scarlet and/or blue with white or cream window frames. This is not a complete picture though, for newspaper reports of the period indicate that two 'coaches' had arrived by September 1863 and languished out of use until the locomotive trials began. These were described by the *Isle of Wight Times* of 17th March, 1864 as a first class double-deck vehicle seating 20 inside and 20 on top and a second class single-deck saloon for 25 passengers (though the opposite class allocations would seem a more logical arrangement). Unfortunately little else is known about them and they seem never to have been used for horse-haulage - presumably because they were too heavy - but they are further evidence that through running over the island's railway system was contemplated from the outset.

The Directors were still considering the use of other forms of motive power besides their horses and, early in 1880 and unperturbed by the imminent curtailing of the line, they commissioned Mr F. Bradley of Glenmore Works, Kidderminster, to adapt the two single-deck tramcars to run on steam. (Bradley was a civil engineer who had carried out work in Ryde, including on the pier.) The original plan was for the steam to be raised by burning coal gas and a small gas holder was erected by the Pier Toll Gate station to store this (supplied by the Ryde Gas Co.) prior to its transfer to bags fitted to the adapted cars. This idea was soon judged to be impractical and the cars were converted to coke-burning and on 7th January, 1881 were delivered in this form. Fitted with vertical boilers, their 4-coupled wheels were driven via a centre jackshaft and side rods. A hand-wheel at each end operated reversing gear. Externally, the wooden bodies were provided with louvres as a means of ventilation in place of the original windows, but internally the temperature remained unbearably high. They ran - though not without their fair share of trouble - until it was considered that the danger of dropped sparks setting the pier alight was too great to allow their continued use. Their weight - approaching 10 tons each - was also a matter for some concern, despite a later 20 per cent reduction. In all, they ran from 31st January, 1881 to 31st October, 1884 with horse traction resuming the next day, and were sold two years later for £42 to the Ryde Gas Co.

The horses, however, were not destined to remain in harness for much longer. Already in 1884 Messrs Blanch, Brain Bros of London had been contracted to modernise the line using electric traction (apparently with battery-powered cars) but it appears that the system to be used had not been perfected and, despite work on it on the pier throughout that summer, no more was heard of the scheme. Consequently, in October 1885, Messrs Siemens Bros of Charlton were contracted to electrify the line, as a railway, on the third-rail system.

Work began immediately on laying a third rail of channel iron on the outward side of the western track, raised on posts 18 in. above the decking. Trials began on Saturday 6th March of the following year using a converted double-deck horse car (reaching speeds of 13 mph) hauling two of the other horse cars. The trials were obviously judged a success for public services began the following week. Current at 120v DC was supplied by a Siemens' SB8 generator driven by a Crossley 16 hp Otto gas engine housed by the pier entrance. In 1889 work began on converting the eastern track and the installation of a second, smaller generating set with a 12 hp engine for one-track working during the winter. This track re-opened the following summer using a 20-seater motor car built by the local firm of Pollard & Sons, each motor car running with a single control trailer that had once been a double-deck horse tram coupled (minus its top deck) to its seaward end. Both motor cars were also single-deck vehicles with closed sides and, like their trailers, apparently unnumbered. A third motor car, possibly also by Pollards, arrived soon afterwards to replace the eastern track's converted horse car. (The remainder of the old fleet was scrapped or otherwise disposed of though one flat wagon was retained for carrying baggage.) A fare of 1d. was charged for a single journey in either direction.

This system of operation, with one pair of cars on each track, lasted until 1927 without major incident (though the Pier Head station was roofed in 1898 some 10 years after a major structural refurbishment of the pier). In October that year the new owner, the Southern Railway (which had acquired the line from the Ryde Pier Co. under its Act of 1924), abandoned the use of electric traction - the cars were now over 40 years old, their trailers even older and the generating plant obsolete - and instead introduced that November two new 4-wheeled

An early postcard view looking past the pier railway station at the pier head along the promenade decking towards the shore, with an electric car in the middle distance. Both station and decking have now been obliterated by a roadway to the ferry terminal on the neighbouring railway pier head. *Author's Collection*

Removing the electric cars, 1st November, 1927, with the 'Grapes' car to the fore. *Lens of Sutton*

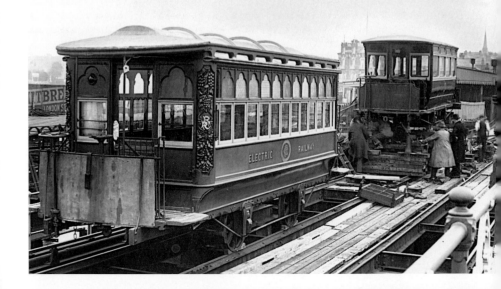

Drewry railcars. Each was powered by a 26 hp Bedford petrol engine via a chain-drive and separate gearboxes for forward and reverse running. Longitudinal seating was provided for 22 with an allowance for 18 standing. The cars, numbered 1 and 2, were closed and their livery dark green. Principal dimensions were: overall length 26 ft 7 in., overall width 7 ft 4 in. and weight 4½ tons. The wheels were 1 ft 11¾ in. in diameter on a 12 ft 6 in. wheelbase. The two electric trailers - No. 3 of 1900 by the Lancaster Railway Carriage & Wagon Co. and No. 4 of 1871 (see below) - were retained for a while and paired with the railcars as before. (No. 4 with railcar 1.) The single fare was now 2*d*. (rising sharply to 6*d*. in 1967).

The major operating difference after the change of traction was that the drivers remained in their railcars throughout a round trip, a method of working which led, in September 1935, to trailer No. 4 (then in use on the western track with railcar No. 2) being propelled at speed right though the stops in the Pier Head station. The damaged trailer was subsequently withdrawn and replaced by trailer No. 7 the following year with No. 3 being replaced by No. 8 in 1937 (both built by the SR at its Eastleigh Works); the flat 4-wheeled luggage truck, now number 5, was withdrawn two years later and replaced by similar vehicle No. 9, built by the SR at Ryde. This latter vehicle was normally kept padlocked to the buffers at the Pier Gates station (as it was now known) for coupling to the western set when needed. No continuous brake was fitted to the stock but in 1937 (on the western track) and 1939 (on the eastern) 100 ft-long ramps were constructed outside each line on the approach to the Pier Head station upon which a small wheel, attached to the railcars, could run. This operated a mechanism whereby a calibrated wooden strip was pushed up in front of the driver's window to indicate just how far away from the stops he was!

The SR-built single-deck trailers were somewhat similar in appearance to the railcars, also having bodies of wood and sheet iron on steel underframes. Weighing 4 tons, their overall length was 26 ft, width 7 ft 5 in. and height 9 ft 9 in. Wheel diameter was also 1 ft 11¾ in., this time on a 10 ft wheelbase. The central compartment, between two vestibules, had longitudinal seats; total (official) accommodation was for 24 seated and 22 standing though, as with the railcars, many more than this would be crammed in if need be.

One of the old trailers happily escaped the scrapheap. This vehicle is the famous 'Grapes Car' - so called on account of the ornately-carved decorations on its bodywork. Trailer No. 4 of the electric railway fleet, it was built for the horse tramway in 1871 by one John Knapp, a local carpenter, with a solid mahogany body mounted on running gear believed to have been supplied by Starbuck. In general outline it was based on the early British tramcar designs of G.F. Train of Birkenhead and London fame and was painted vermillion with blue panelling, with the eponymous wooden fruit a beautiful shade of deep purple. The interior was gilded and mats were even provided for pasengers to wipe their feet on before entry! It was converted to a trailer for electric working by the removal of the upper deck fittings; after running with the petrol railcars until its 1935 accident, its remains were purchased by tramway enthusiast and campaigner H.C. Winstone of Romford and donated to the Hull Transport Museum (where it is erroneously numbered 3).

One of the two 1927 Drewry railcars, plus a former electric trailer, running after the abandonment of electric traction. Beyond is the 1881 railway pier.   *R.W. Kidner*

A Drewry railcar again, this time coupled with one of the 1930s purpose-built trailers, outside the pier head station on 21st April, 1957.   *T.J. Edgington*

A similar - if not identical - pairing in service on 18th May, 1964. The signal is for the railway pier line.   *T.J. Edgington*

A crowded Pier Gates station on 17th August, 1969. Just visible to the left is part of Ryde Esplanade railway station.   *T.J. Edgington*

Before the 1969 closure: the ornate entrance to the two-platform Pier Head station . . .

Lens of Sutton

. . . and its somewhat less prepossessing landward facade.   *R.W. Kidner*

After Nationalisation the line passed into the ownership and control of British Railways, who continued to operate it much as before. In 1959-60 the railcars' Bedford engines were replaced by Perkins diesel engines and ran without further change until 1969 when the line suffered the same fate as that already experienced by much of the island's railway system: closure. On Friday 30th December, 1966 the last steam trains had run on the island and, after the necessary conversion work had been carried out, from Monday 20th March, 1967 a service of ex-London Underground stock had been provided from the adjoining railway pier head to Shanklin - all that was left of the island's once intensive standard gauge system. So as to eliminate competition, the unpopular decision was taken to close the pier line and on Sunday 26th January, 1969 the last train ran, made up of railcar No. 2 and trailer No. 7, to be replaced by a shuttle service on the railway pier. That March and April the line's stock - with one exception - was broken up for disposal at Ryde Esplanade by Jolliffe of Cowes, scrap merchants.

The exception to the scrapping of the stock was railcar No. 2 which was acquired by the Wight Locomotive Society. Minus its bodywork, it was moved by road to Newport in February 1969; from there it travelled on Sunday 24th January, 1971 - under its own power - to Haven Street for possible use on the Isle of Wight Steam Railway as a permanent way vehicle. It was in fact the last vehicle to leave Newport station before the track was lifted. One other former item of stock has since been rescued: in 1979 the body of the 1889 Pollard electric car was purchased at a farm sale by Bernard Pratt, a former county councillor, and sent to the IoW College of Arts & Technology for restoration. After completion of the task in December 1985 it was transferred to the Cothry Bottom Heritage centre at Westridge near Ryde where it stands, nicknamed 'Polly', as the main exhibit in a pier display. At its original home the 700 yards of track remained until re-decking work in the early 1970s, a mute reminder of a tramway that was challenged, and defeated, by a railway. Now only the bare girders are left where it once ran, whilst the other half of the pier is a roadway to the pier head.

Looking towards the tramway and railway pier heads before the former line was closed and the latter electrified. A pair of Isle of Wight tanks wait to depart for Ryde Esplanade and beyond.
Lens of Sutton

Although the tramway (*foreground*) closed in 1969, services on the railway pier survive and are now operated by ex-London tube trains   *P.G. Barnes*

Chapter Seven

Southend-on-Sea Pier Tramway and Railways

Not only is it the longest pier in this country, Southend pier is the longest such structure in the world and its railway is the busiest and most famous of such lines. The present pier dates from 1889 but prior to its construction the site was occupied by an earlier structure also boasting a system of rail transport which, like the pier, gradually evolved with time.

Work was begun on the first pier on 25th July, 1829 by the Southend Pier Co. under its Act of that year, one of the principal movers of the scheme being a local resident and former Lord Mayor of London, Alderman (later Sir) William Heygate. Built entirely of wood, the first completed section of some 500 ft opened in June of the following year whilst further construction continued. By 1835 the pier had reached a length of ½ mile but even then boat passengers had to travel a further ¼ mile on foot or by cart at low tide in order to reach small boats which would ferry them to the 'pier head' - an old moored vessel later replaced by a pile structure known as the Mount. The width of the pier was 20 ft for the first 200 yards, after which it tapered to 8 ft. By 1846 the pier had reached deep water with a length of 1¼ miles, making it the longest in Europe, but was in another sort of deep water - financial - and that same year it was mortgaged to the Public Works Loan Commission who in turn sold it to Mr Waddington, the then Chairman of the Eastern Counties Railway, for £17,000 (it had cost some £40-50,000 to build). This period of ownership saw the laying of the first line along the pier for the purpose of conveying the luggage of steamer passengers. This was a single track down the east side of the pier and was served by three hand-propelled trucks. It was probably unique among pier lines in that the rails (laid to an unrecorded but approximately 3 ft 6 in. gauge) were of wood. Less unusual for pier lines was a special sail-fitted truck for use if and when the wind was favourable - a counterpart to that used at Herne Bay during the same period (*see Chapter Three*).

The ownership of both pier and tramway changed hands another two times before being offered to the Local Board for £12,000 at the end of 1873 and eventually sold to it, a price of £10,000 having been agreed. It was decided by the new owner to adapt the line for passenger transport and the wooden rails were accordingly replaced with flat-bottomed iron ones spiked directly to the decking. Three small enclosed carriages (somewhat reminiscent of the Festiniog Railway's original 4-wheelers) were provided; they were possibly adaptations of the old luggage trucks. The line's fourth vehicle was a small flat truck coupled at the seaward end of the rake of carriages to which the driver's seat was fitted. The whole tram was pulled by two horses in tandem (originally only one was used) and ran straight through the entertainments pavilion on the pier - a regular feature of any concert or the like held there was sounding of a warning bell followed by the clip-clopping, creaking progress of the tram through the tent with majestic disinterest in the proceedings which were being so rudely interrupted!

47

The splendid entrance to Southend pier, and pavilion, depicted on a pre-World War I postcard.
Author's Collection

A postcard of the first electric railway on the pier with a rake of early cars by the end of the ramp
up to the upper decking at the shore end.   *Author's Collection*

This touch of the ridiculous seems characteristic of the line, for in the year after its opening one town councillor ventured that since the horses' hooves showed an alarming tendency to slip through holes in the decking, might not elephants be gainfully employed instead? In fact, the truth was that the line had been too flimsily-constructed for the amount of wear and tear it was receiving: despite wearing rubber shoes, the horses wore holes in the planks and the extremely lightweight rails spread and twisted. After a life of only six years the numerous 15-minute journeys had taken their toll and the line was forced to close, leaving the Board with a serious drop in revenue from the pier.

The situation remained unaltered for a further four years until the decision to rebuild the pier completely was made in August 1885, this time using iron piles as supports. Two years later the necessary Act of Parliament was secured and it was decided to install a modern electric railway as part of the new pier's amenities. Construction began in 1888, the contractors being Messrs Arrol Bros of Glasgow, and took two years to complete. The main section of the pier was 2,000 yds long and 30 ft wide, erected alongside the old structure, with the pier head built on timber piles at the end. Although not finished, it was opened to the public in 1889 and work began on the railway the following year when the decking was complete enough to take it, under the supervision of Mr C.E. Norton, the former electrical engineer on the pier. The actual installation work was carried out by Messrs Crompton & Co. Ltd of Chelmsford while the overall construction was carried out under the supervision of the Southend Local Board's Engineer, Dr Hopkinson.

The line was laid as a single track down the east side of the pier with 45 lb. flat-bottomed rails spiked to 12 in. x 4½ in. longitudinal sleepers. The gauge was 3 ft 6 in. and a centre rail laid to supply the electricity. This 'rail' was actually a steel channel and copper strip on petticoat insulators and was fed with current at 200v DC from a generator belt-driven by a Davey & Paxman 25 hp compound steam engine (with locomotive-type boiler). The sole original car (No. 1) was supplied by the Falcon Works of Loughborough and was equipped with a 13 hp Crompton motor. Current pick-up was via a carbon brush contact onto the live rail. In appearance it was a 4-wheeled tramcar with open sides, end platforms and curved dashboards lettered (variously, or at different dates) SOUTHEND LOCAL BOARD 1 and SOUTHEND LOCAL BOARD CROMPTON ELECTRIC RAILWAY. Internally it was fitted with six rows of cross-bench seats. Livery was green.

Pier and railway were opened officially on Saturday 2nd August, 1890, although the railway had not been completed with only ¾ mile as yet laid. Total expenditure on the project had been £80,000 in all, of which £11,080 was for the railway. The first official trip along the line was made that afternoon (after a delay of several hours) when half the Local Board, Dr Hopkinson and Col R.E.B. Crompton all squeezed into the car for a brisk 10-minute round trip.

Public working commenced at 4.00 pm on the following day, and between that time and dusk some 800 passengers were carried; from that day on the line's popularity grew and grew and the solitary car was kept busy for the rest of the season plying a 4-minute service from end to end. So immediate in fact was the line's popularity that two more cars (Nos. 2 and 3), both unpowered cross-bench vehicles, were purchased in 1891 in time for the completion of the

The Pier, Showing Electric Trams, Southend-on-Sea.

A.W. Judd & Co.
Southend.

Two five-coach trains in the pier head station prior to the commencement of the track-doubling programme. The message on the back of the postcard reads: 'Daisy, Ray & I went to the end of the pier yesterday morning, on the tram. It was so windy, Ray lost his cap.'

Author's Collection

track to the pier head - a total distance of 1¼ miles. These two cars were used as trailers for the original car, all three working as a single set.

In 1893 the Corporation (Southend having become a Borough the previous year) purchased another set of three cars (Nos. 4-6) similar to the first, again from the Falcon Works.

The idea of installing a centre loop was first put forward in 1896, thus enabling the two sets to work in opposition, but nothing came of the plan until 1898 after a new extension and pier head were opened (necessitated by the silting round the old pier head). The loop - just long enough for the two trains to pass - was opened in July 1898 at a cost of £4,100 and lengthened during the following year as a result of the purchase of a further six cars. These came from the Brush Electrical Engineering Co. Ltd, the successor to Falcon, and were similar cross-bench vehicles (presumably numbered 7-12) comprising a motor car, two ordinary trailers and three control trailers or 'leaders'; these were used to make the fleet up to three trains, each of four cars. A second engine and generator were also installed on the pier at the same time to cope with the increased demand for electricity.

By now the railway was going from strength to strength as the service was continually expanded and improved to deal with the ever-growing traffic. In 1902 the stock was added to once again with the purchase of four new trailers from Brush; at the same time the complete generating plant was disposed of and the line connected to the town supply of 500v DC. Two new 18 hp General Electric motors were fitted to each of the three motor cars in place of the old 13 hp one - an increase in power reflecting the amount of work now required of the cars. At the same time the car fleet underwent a number of changes with the original No. 1 being converted into a powered luggage wagon (unnumbered), two of the older trailers (1891 and 1893 vintage) being rebuilt at Southend with GE motors as enclosed cars 6 and 10 and the surviving open trailers were lengthened by Brush to accommodate four more passengers on end platform seats. (All the motor cars were later enclosed.)   Other cars were then renumbered to fill the gaps, producing the following passenger stock list:

No. 1:	Control trailer of 1902
No. 2:	Trailer of 1891
No. 3:	Motor car of 1899
No. 4:	Control trailer of 1893
No. 5:	Trailer of 1893
No. 6:	Closed motor car of 1902 rebuild
Nos. 7-9:	Control trailers of 1899
No. 10:	Closed motor car of 1902 rebuild
Nos. 11, 12:	Trailers of 1899
Nos. 13-15:	Control trailers of 1902
No. 16:	Motor car of 1902

This meant that four trains of four cars could now be operated, each with one motor car, two leaders and one ordinary trailer, though after a period of seven years it was decided that yet more stock was need and accordingly a further five Brush trailers were acquired, No. 17 being a saloon trailer for winter use, Nos. 18 and 19 open cross-bench control trailers and Nos. 20 and 21 similar ordinary trailers. With five cars now in a summer train, this meant imposing a further

A later, seven-coach train of pre-1949 electric stock, open-sided and closed. Motor car No. 3 leads.
H.C. Casserley

One of the old winter cars in operation, 15th January, 1949, with colour light signals to the fore and signal box and crossover in the distance.
J.H. Meredith, courtesy Lens of Sutton

load on the motors and in 1910 they were replaced by 27 hp GE ones, again two to each car. At the same time work began on extending the line's North (at the shore end of the pier) and South stations. This work was spread over the following five years and cost £7,210 altogether.

Traffic figures for this period were well over the 75,000 mark each year and in 1912 four more Brush cross-bench trailers (Nos. 22-25) were added to stock, followed by four more (Nos. 26-29) in 1913, the fleet then being reorganised into four rakes of seven cars each for summer workings. All rakes were alike, consisting of a motor car (in the centre) together with three control trailers and three non-driving trailers. The leaders were fitted with BTH controllers; the motor car was actually non-driving on account of its position with regard to forward vision. The extra leader in each rake meant that if traffic was light, two of the trailers at the seaward end would be detached leaving a rake of five - the minimum number allowed - still with a leader at each end. The braking system was mechanical in operation and was worked by means of hand controls in the front and rear cars. (Magnetic brakes were in fact fitted to one rake in 1923 for experimental trials, but later discarded.)

One of the 1912 trailers (possibly No. 25) was rebuilt as a semi-open petrol-electric winter car soon after its arrival and renumbered 31; this was joined in 1914 by similar car 32, though whether this was a new vehicle or another rebuild is uncertain. Both were later converted to third-rail operation. Each seated 30 passengers, was equipped with an old 18 hp motor and had controllers at both ends.

The unladen weight of the motor cars was 5 tons 15 cwt and that of the trailers 4 tons; overall length was 22 ft 9 in. to 24 ft, height 6 ft 11 in. to 7 ft 3 in., width about 6 ft 5 in. and wheelbase 6 ft 9 in. to 11 ft 6 in. according to the different age and type of vehicle. A train of seven cars was capable of carrying 200-300 passengers (including standees) on each trip - a considerable number compared to any of the other pier lines.

Two other vehicles completed the rolling stock fleet. Both service vehicles, one was the railway's original No. 1, now a motorised platform car for carrying luggage and stores to the steamers (during the summer season of 1914 steamers called at the pier at the rate of 10 a day) and numbered 29 whilst the other (No. 30) was a simple flat trailer carrying a water tank, again for serving the steamers. Both cars ran together and separate from the rest of the stock.

No further additions or major changes were made to the fleet until after World War II; attention instead was focused upon the task of improving the facilities of the pier in general and of the railway in particular. The problem was one of efficiency: how could the line's stock (vast by pier railway standards) be most effectively utilised without further expenditure on new cars? The obvious and logical solution was to double-track the line, although curiously it was several years before this was finally completed.

In 1921 the line received its first royal visit when King George V visited the pier on 14th July during Yachting Week and one of the cars was specially decked-out for the occasion. The King repeated his visit two years later, and during that same year the job of renewing the wheels of all the cars was begun. This work lasted until 1925, by which time all the stock had been fitted with new wheels clad with Bessemer steel tyres.

In 1926 the Pier Committee put forward proposals for adapting the railway to deal with the ever-increasing numbers of prospective passengers (annual figures were now nudging the 2 million mark) by extending the double track out from each station and lengthening the centre loop. The Southend Pier Order of 1927 was accordingly obtained for this purpose and in the following year the centre passing-loop was extended a further 150 yards and the double-track section at each end of the line also lengthened. The year 1928 also saw the line's most serious accident - happily without tragic consequences. On Thursday 20th September, at about 4.00 pm, a northbound train was entering the passing loop when the last two cars were struck by a southbound train leaving the loop - apparently the result of a sudden attack of illness on the part of its driver. The two cars were derailed violently and flung onto the railings separating the railway from the rest of the decking. Seven cars in all were damaged, the water main along the pier broken, and other minor structural damage occasioned. Luckily, as soon as the collision occurred, the electricity was automatically switched off. The two trains were only lightly loaded at the time and, incredibly, no-one was seriously injured. A makeshift service was operating only three hours later for those unperturbed enough to make the trip.

Just how astonishingly busy the pier was during the inter-war period can be gauged from the record admissions for a Sunday recorded on 15th July, 1928: a total of 31,280 with 16,547 steamer passengers landing or embarking.

The task of completing the track-doubling was finally started in 1929 by the Titan Trackwork Co. of Sheffield. Earlier that year, on 8th July, Prince George, Duke of Kent, travelled over the line to open the new extension to the pier head, also built under the 1927 Order and named after him. The track was doubled by extending the centre and station loops until they met. A scissors crossover with facing point locks was installed some 200 yards out from each station and a signal box erected on the seaward side of each crossover. Each housed a 7-lever manual frame for the points and new, semi-automatic, colour light signals installed by the Westinghouse Brake & Saxby Signalling Co. The points could be locked-off for single-line working, which later became the norm. In each station the tracks diverged slightly round an island platform. All the rails used were 45 lb. flat-bottomed ones - the original steel channel conductor rail had been replaced with one identical to the running rails in 1911 (whilst at the same time iron shoes replaced the old carbon brush contacts) and in 1919 all rails (both running and conductor) had been renewed. Total cost of the doubling and signalling was £35,000 and working over the new line began the following Whitsun. Trains to the pier head used the eastern track and returning trains the western.

During the winter of 1931-32 a completely new entrance to the pier was built to replace the old one which had been demolished two years before. The year 1935 saw the pier celebrate its centenary and the railway ran a special train for the Mayor and Mayoress and various visiting dignitaries for the unveiling of a commemorative plaque at the pier head by the chairman of the Port of London Authority, Lord Ritchie of Dundee, on Tuesday 23rd July.

Before any more major changes could be implemented, war broke out once more and the pier was immediately taken over by the Royal Navy. Concrete and barbed wire was the order of the day as fortifications were erected and anti-aircraft guns mounted in position. The railway was naturally taken over too, lock, stock and barrel to make its own small but important contribution to the war effort. Several of the cars were converted to 'ambulances' and ran round the clock ferrying wounded from ship to shore, as well as large numbers of able-bodied survivors from stricken ships, and load upon load of stores and equipment - despite chronic staff shortages and the ensuing lack of maintenance.

The pier and railway re-opened to the public in May 1945 with the end of hostilities in Europe, and by 1947 annual traffic figures were over the 3 million mark. The strains and stresses of the war years and the ever-increasing number of passengers - over 4½ million in 1949 - was now being felt by the rolling-stock and the decision was taken to renew the entire passenger car fleet. An order was therefore placed with A.C. Cars Ltd of Thames Ditton for four complete trains of seven coaches each - 12 motor cars and 16 trailers altogether. The total cost was £112,000 and the principal sub-contractors for the work were in fact Messrs Crompton Parkinson Ltd, the successors to the original railway builders.

The first of the new trains arrived in March 1949 and a formal inauguration took place on Wednesday 13th April when the official maiden trip was made by Lord Broadbridge in the company of various Corporation members and other officials and dignitaries. The Mayor of Southend himself was at the controls of one of the new rakes for the trip from the pier head to the shore, the outward journey having been made in one of the old trains. That evening saw the official switching-on of the pier illuminations after the blackout of the war years.

The new cars were, in design, very advanced for their time, and included several new features later to be adopted by the London Underground. Each train was formed of three motor cars and four trailers, one motor car being marshalled at each end of the rake and the third in the middle. Each rake could be controlled from either end cab and operated as a single unit (although individual motor cars were sometimes used when traffic was exceptionally light, or for shunting purposes). No less than three braking systems were fitted: electric rheostatic for main use, air-operated brakes for bringing the train to a halt in the stations, and a hand brake for parking. All the cars were 4-wheeled, like the old stock, and identical in external appearance with totally enclosed bodywork that reached down nearly level with the rails. Passenger boarding was via a centre entrance with two sliding, air-operated doors - the system adopted for use on the London Underground. The large side windows, together with the curved side roof lights provided the passenger-visibility of open cars in the comfort of closed stock. The motor cars were numbered 1, 4, 7, 8, 11, 14, 15, 18, 21, 22, 25 and 28 with the missing numbers being taken by the trailers.

Seating was for 38 in the trailers, on transverse seats, whilst the motor cars held 31 on both transverse and longitudinal seats. All cars were equipped with central buffers and spring draw gear with their bodies mounted on leaf springs and rubber suspension units. Dimensions for both types of car were the same: length 29 ft 6 in., height 7 ft 9 in., width 6 ft 6 in. Wheels were 2 ft in diameter and set at a 14 ft 6 in. wheelbase - surprisingly long but chosen for stability, and possible because of the absence of sharp curves on the railway. Maximum speed was 18 mph and the livery green with cream lower end panels and side stripes.

A contrast in design: old and new trains together at the North station, 1949.

J.H. Meredith, courtesy Lens of Sutton

A postcard issued to mark the railway's diamond jubilee celebrations of 20th-27th May, 1950 showing one of the new A.C. Cars trains at the North station.   *Author's Collection*

In the year of its introduction the new stock carried over 4,700,000 passengers with the old stock phased out of service as the new trains commenced their duties. Two of the 1899 driving trailers were sold to the Volk's Electric Railway at Brighton to be converted and regauged as motor cars (Nos. 8 and 9) on the 2 ft 8½ in. line along the beach there, and continue their lives within another pebble's throw of the sea (although both are out of service at the time of writing). The rest of the old passenger stock was disposed of, presumably as scrap of one form or another - though not lost totally (*see below*).

The new cars provided an excellent, trouble-free service though passenger figures began to drop steadily from their 1949 peak until the late 1960s, when the annual returns showed an average of 1½ million a year. When this figure fell below 1 million in 1970 (by which date steamer dockings had virtually ceased) services were reduced by halving the number of passenger cars in active use and reorganising working. The crossovers were lifted and the signalling removed with services operated thereafter by two trains, one permanently assigned to each now separate line. Cars Nos. 1-7 worked the east line while Nos. 22-25, 17, 27 and 28 (renumbered 8-14) worked the west. Of the remaining 14 cars, Nos. 11, 14, 15, 20 and 21 went into a storage limbo for possible disposal, or use in rotation with the others to even out tyre wear, whilst (old) Nos. 9, 10, 12, 13, 16, 18, 19 and 26 were dismantled for spares with one of the bodies being sold for £1 to a railway driver for use as a garden shed - a familiar story in the history of railway and tramway rolling stock! No. 8 was converted into a single-cab flat-bed works car as a replacement for No. 29 of the old stock.

The two covered stations remained unaltered, the North station (beneath the Pier Pavilion beyond the actual entrance to the pier) housing the line's lifting facilities and inspection pits; beneath this in turn were sited the pier's general workshops where repairs and maintenance to the cars was also undertaken.

After a child fell through the decking in 1971 it was discovered that the pier was in need of drastic refurbishment, though in view of its length to keep it open without some form of transport along it was unthinkable and in 1972 it was announced that Mitchell Ropeways, a British Ropes subsidiary, was to supply the Swiss-designed 'Aerobus' passenger transport system to replace the railway. This would have entailed erecting pylons beside the pier, linked by steel cables from which would be hung two 100-seater passenger cars - in effect a horizontal cable-car system. In the event the idea was dropped and the line which had survived the war bombardment and two breachings in peacetime (by the concrete motor schooner *Violette* on 18th January, 1921 and by the barge *Matilda* on 17th March, 1933), as well as other minor damage by shipping, soldiered on for another four years. (The first pier, incidentally, was also breached when the barge *West Kent* was driven through it in the great gale of January 1881.) Instead, it was decided in 1974 to single the line as a means of reducing costs, commencing in 1975 with the work to be spread over 15 years. That year saw the delivery (by floating crane) of an Atlas/PAPE 5000SP self-propelled hydraulic crane for use in the work. Weighing 8 tons and capable of lifting 6.6 tons, it was equipped with retractable wheels so as to spread its weight evenly along the rails under its 16 ft length. It was followed in February 1976 by a 4-wheeled Wickham petrol railcar for the use of the Corporation's

One of the 1949 seven-coach trains *en route* to the pier head.

H.C. *Casserley, courtesy Lens of Sutton*

Two 1949 trains passing outside the South station.   *Author's Collection*

One of the 1949 trains inside the South station at the pier head. *Lens of Sutton*

South station on 14th June, 1970 with motor car 28 on its train (shortly before it was renumbered 14). *T.J. Edgington*

Looking towards the shore from South station on 14th June, 1970 with motor car 1 nearest the camera.   *T.J. Edgington*

The two 1899 driving trailers sold to the Volks Electric Railway, Brighton in 1949 seen in their guises of Nos. 8 and 9 there on 9th August, 1970.   *T.J. Edgington*

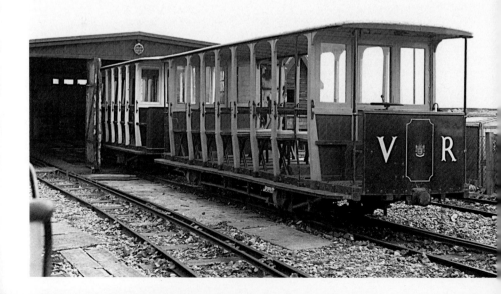

workforce. The western track was in fact closed to passenger trains from 1974 onwards, to be used by workers redecking the adjacent pier area.

Matters were not helped when, on Thursday 29th July, 1976, much of the pier head was destroyed by fire with the railway (luckily unaffected) used to rescue visitors and provide back-up to the emergency services. When reconstruction work on the pier commenced it was discovered that singling the line would be a pointless exercise since the track had come to the end of its safe working life and, from 1st October, 1978, the railway was accordingly closed. Within four years the entire stock and other equipment had been sold or otherwise disposed of - no tender for the purchase of the railway as a whole had been judged acceptable and at the end of 1980 it had been taken off the market. Two of the passenger cars (Nos. 7 and 21) and works car No. 8 were bought privately for the embryonic North Wales Tramway Museum near Llandudno for possible use on a pleasure line, or as a source of parts in the restoration of older tramcars. The hydraulic crane and Wickham railcar went to the Brecon Mountain Railway for regauging to 1 ft 11¾ in. and service as engineering works vehicles. (The pier railway's wheel-turning lathe also went to the BMR and can be seen in its workshop.) The electrical supply equipment was bought by the East Anglia Transport Museum, near Lowestoft, to help operate its tramway and trolleybuses.

For several years it seemed that the pier was destined to remain trainless but in 1985 the firm of May, Gurney (Colchester) Ltd was contracted to lay a new, 3 ft gauge railway from shore to pier head (with Motor Rail diesel locomotive No. 10160 of 1950 used during construction); an official 'track re-opening' ceremony was held on Tuesday 17th September that year, after which the old track was lifted and 35 tons of rail sold to the Dowty Railway Society for use on their narrow gauge line at Toddington in Gloucestershire. This is the railway operating today: a single track, with a midway passing loop and two terminal roads at each end, laid with 35 lb. flat-bottomed rails clipped to steel sleepers, every fifth one of which is spiked to the new decking along the centre of the pier. (The supporting timbers for the old line were removed, thus reducing the width of the pier by a third between the stations and the passing loop.) A siding from the North station to workshops on the same level completes the layout. Semi-automatic colour light signals for the passing loop are controlled from the North station and the length of the line is 2,180 yards. Total cost of construction was £1½ million.

Two six-car trains (with carriages numbered A1-6 and B1-6) were supplied in March 1986 by the Severn Lamb Engineering Co. of Stratford-upon-Avon, each consisting of a motor car at the seaward end (A1 or B1), four trailers then a driving trailer (A6 or B6), all enclosed bogie vehicles. The power unit is a Deutz 55 hp diesel engine powering Linde hydraulic motors in the bogies, with chain final drives to the axles, giving a top speed of 18 mph, though the speed limit imposed by the Department of Transport is 10 mph. Air-brakes are fitted to supplement the braking provided by the hydraulic drive and the livery is maroon with white stripes. Passenger accommodation, on longitudinal fibreglass seats, is in the central trailers (24 seated with room for 10 standing) and the control trailers (12 seating plus pram and wheelchair area) only, giving a total of 182 passengers per train. Access is by central sliding doors controlled

The new Severn-Lamb cars being unloaded at the pier in 1986 . . .   *Severn-Lamb Ltd*

. . . and one of the two new trains posed for a publicity shot on the rebuilt railway.
Severn-Lamb Ltd

by the drivers, who are in radio contact with each other and the North station. Principal dimensions of the cars, which have aluminium bodies mounted on steel chassis, are:

Length (motor cars):	20 ft 9 in.
Length (control trailers):	20 ft 9 in.
Length (ordinary trailers)	20 ft
Width:	5 ft 9 in.
Height:	7 ft 6 in.
Weight (motor cars):	4 tons
Weight (trailers):	2 tons

The one goods vehicle is a 30 ft bogie flat wagon used to service the pier head facilities (a task which includes ferrying supplies out to the 'Jolly Fisherman' pub there) and propelled by one of the trains when required.

The new line was officially opened on Friday 2nd May, 1986 by the Princess Royal who named the motor car of train A *Sir John Betjeman* in commemoration of the Poet Laureate, who had died two years previously and whose favourite pier Southend was. Train B is named *Sir William Heygate*. That same day Brent Walker (Leisure) Ltd took over the running of the pier and railway on behalf of the Council. (This arrangement lasted two years only though and the line is now once more operated directly by the local authority.) During the first week of operation over 10,000 passengers were carried (some 6,500 on the May Day Bank Holiday alone) with a fare of £1 return for adults and 60p for children. On Wednesday 7th June, 1995 the pier was again damaged by fire, this time at the shore end, with the railway suffering some track buckling from the heat. A temporary terminus was therefore opened short of the North station for the electric trains and a battery railcar was ordered from Castleline of Nottingham to work a shuttle service between these two points (and a winter service along the whole railway). Numbered 1835 - to commemorate the year the pier first appeared on Admiralty charts - this is a three-axle, double-ended vehicle with central doors.

The current railway fare is £1.85 for a round trip with one train in use at all times to provide a basic half-hour service with the other set brought out if traffic demand warrants it.

Mention has been made above of the Pier Museum. This is housed below the North station in the old workshops and, amongst other artefacts and exhibits, is home to three of the 1949 passenger cars (Nos. 2 and 11 rescued from a scrapyard at Shoebury and No. 22 saved from a similar fate in Chelmsford), plus the old motor flat wagon (No. 29) which it is planned to restore to its original 1890 toast-rack form using a body salvaged from a Benfleet garden. Opened on 8th July, 1989, the museum is controlled by a Pier Museum Trust and is a commendable sign of the way piers must adapt and advance in order to earn their keep today. In 1991 one of the old pier signal boxes was reconstructed here and a long-term possibility is to use at least some of the stock on some form of pleasure line along the town's seafront. The museum is currently open Fridays to Mondays, from May to October.

An illustration from *The Graphic* of 12th October, 1872 showing one of the two cable cars on the occasion of the visit of Princess Mary and the Duke of Teck to Southport pier.

A pre-World War I postcard of the electric railway with the three 1905 cars operating as a train.
Author's Collection

On the Pier, Southport

Chapter Eight

Southport Pier Tramway and Railways

Southport, Lancashire, was the site of the first iron pier ever built in the British Isles. The original structure was 1,465 yds long and opened in 1860 by the Southport Pier Co. Its length meant the need for a tramway was soon felt and the installation of one was accordingly authorised by the Directors; the line duly opened to the public on Thursday 7th May, 1863 and was an immediate success. As regards operation, the line was simplicity itself: a single track ran the length of the pier down the centre of the decking, and hand-propelled along this was the tramway's one carriage. The popularity of the pier was at once enhanced at a stroke by this facility - so much so in fact that on 5th December of the same year the Directors decided to widen the pier, move the tramway to the south side and rebuild it as a railway with cable traction. Further details of the tramway's stock and operations are sadly lacking.

The 2,400 yds of cable needed was purchased from Messrs Newall & Co. of Gateshead and Liverpool and was of 1¼ in. diameter. Power was supplied by an 8 hp stationary engine built for the line at a cost of £220 by Messrs Routledge & Ommanney of Salford. The remainder of the necessary machinery was obtained from Messrs Rothwell of Bolton and work commenced during 1864 on widening the pier and installing the winding apparatus. The winding house was sited midway along the pier and connected with the station at each end of the line by means of a telegraph. Two carriages were supplied by the North of England Carriage Co. of Preston, each being a very long, open car with a very high centre knifeboard seat split in two by the mid-side entrance. Wooden balustrades formed the sides and up to 50 passengers could be accommodated on the four wooden benches in each car. The two cars were coupled together, attached fore and aft to the ends of the cable and hauled along the line in funicular fashion. The 1,188 yds-journey from shore to pier head normally took three minutes to complete and afforded a leisurely and effortless ride along the pier with unencumbered views over the railings on either side of the line. Public operation started in 1865 (exact date unknown), making it the first (self-contained) cable line to be constructed for passenger traffic in the world, easily predating the Highgate Hill cable tramway in London of 1884, the 1875 South Cliff funicular railway at Scarborough and even the first (1873) of the famous San Francisco cable tramways.

Sadly, tragedy struck on 1st August, 1865 soon after the opening. The following contemporary account gives the unhappy story:

On Tuesday evening an accident of a serious character happened on the Southport pier. The tramway carriages started from the pier head shortly after five o'clock and proceeded until within about 200 yards of the engine house, when the hindermost carriage left the rails, and ran against the iron and woodwork which separates the tramway from the footpath. Fortunately there were only two persons on the carriage at the time, Mrs Bateman of Liverpool and her son- or brother-in law, Mr Atherton, both of whom received severe injuries, their legs being crushed and torn between the railings and the carriage on which they were seated. The woodwork was broken for a

An early view of the pier with the pre-1937 stock in the shore station.

Boots Pure Drug Co. Ltd

considerable distance, and the footboard of the carriage was also smashed. The injured parties were conveyed to the Victoria Hotel, where Mrs Bateman, who had received frightful injuries to her legs, died yesterday. Her son-in-law is unable to leave his bed. The cause of the accident is unknown.   (*Sheffield Independent* 4th August, 1865)

After the necessary repairs had been carried out the line was inspected by Col Yolland on behalf of the Board of Trade in an attempt to prevent a repetition of the accident. Happily, no other serious accident has marred the line's history since. The inspection was carried out on 5th March, 1866 and the line passed as fit for public usage. Operation recommenced and continued without change for nearly 30 years until 1893 when the line closed for the second major upheaval in its life. During this period it received a visit from royalty, the following contemporary account providing a fitting commentary:

On the 9th of October, 1872, the pier was honoured by a visit from HRH the Princess Mary of Cambridge, her illustrious husband the Duke of Teck, and a fashionable coterie. A carriage had been most elegantly fitted up for the accommodation of the distinguished guests, to whom an address was read by the chairman of the company.
(*New Illustrated Guide to Southport and Neighbourhood* 1873)

Obviously a very proud moment for the Directors!

In 1893 (the same year that saw the incorporation of the Southport Pier Co. as a limited company) the line was re-opened after conversion to the tramway system of cable haulage with driver-controlled grippers on the cars engaging with an otherwise unattached, continually-moving cable. New winding engines were supplied by Wilkinson & Co. Ltd of Wigan and the entire permanent way relaid. New, covered cars were also provided; the journey time remained the same. The Board of Trade again inspected the line and again sanctioned its re-opening. The railway continued in this form for another 12 years before the next major change took place. In 1899 it was proposed to double the line but the work was never carried out. The gauge of the line for both periods of cable operation was 3 ft 6 in. and it is probable that the gauge of the 1863 line was the same.

The next major change was the electrification of the line on the third-rail system by the British Westinghouse Co. The line was retained in its same position and a third rail laid (in accordance with normal pier railway practice) on the seaward side. This rail was fed with current at 500v DC taken directly from the town supply. Now shortened to 1,079 yards, the railway re-opened on Monday 3rd April, 1905 and was operated with a stock of three bogie carriages: one motor saloon and two trailers. The motor saloon was a closed vehicle with an arched roof (which gave it an appearance closely resembling that of an early London tube carriage) and was powered by two 30 hp Westinghouse motors. The two trailers were similar in appearance, but roofless. The motor saloon was fitted with controllers at each end on small platforms and the trailers likewise at the outer ends, though these were later removed and the rake controlled from the centre. It seems probably that the set was a rebuild of the old cable cars (or the trailers were at least) with new bodies on the old underframes. According to the demands of traffic, the motor saloon was used by itself or with either or both of the trailers. Each car carried a maximum of 88 passengers, 60 seated and the rest standing.

The modernised (1937) electric set with the train crew in spotless uniforms in keeping with the new stock.   *Lens of Sutton*

The 1953 *Silver Belle*, in the late 1960s, outside the shore station.   *C.H. Loker*

On the day of the re-opening over 50 trips were made and the summer service began with running from 8 am to 10 pm, internal electric lighting being fitted to the cars. Service during the winter season lasted from 8 am until dusk.

Operation continued uneventfully (the fare went up from 1*d*. to 2*d*. in 1928) until 1936 when Southport Corporation purchased the line from the Southport Pier Co. Ltd, which went into voluntary liquidation in February of the following year, and immediately set about the urgent task of renovating and repairing the line. The local firm of Hill Brothers was contracted to equip the old underframes with three new bodies based on the design of the new Blackpool single-sided trams (built by the English Electric Co. Ltd at Preston). Accordingly, the bodies of a closed motor saloon and two high-sided and high-ended open trailers were produced and the old underframes lengthened to receive them. The rebuilt stock ran for two seasons only in this form, for in 1939 the cars were fitted with new Metrovick motors and controllers. The manner of working was as before. The green and cream livery was also copied from the Blackpool trams, but only after the Corporation's original scheme for silvered steel panels was found to be impractical owing to the corrosive effects of sea spray.

In 1950 the production of DC electricity in the town ceased, leaving the Corporation Pier Committee with the choice of either installing a rectifier (and if necessary re-wiring the electrical equipment) to make use of the town's lower AC supply, or converting the line to a completely different form of traction. The decision was made to adopt the latter course of action, and it was agreed to implement a plan proposed by Councillor Barlow, the owner of the Southport Lakeside Miniature Railway (originally a Narrow Gauge Railways venture built in 1915 to a 15 in. gauge), to replace the existing pier line with a 60 cm (1 ft 11½ in.) gauge miniature railway. This plan was put into action immediately and the old line and stock scrapped. The new track was laid with 55 lb. flat-bottomed rails spiked to 10 in. x 10 in. longitudinal sleepers supported on rolled-steel joists which were in turn bolted to the girders of the pier. The track layout consisted of a single line with a two-track station at the shore end.

The new railway opened to the public on Saturday 27th May, 1950 and ran for 900 yards along the 1,211 yds-long pier (the original structure had been shortened when it was rebuilt but it is still the second-longest pier in England) and was worked by a Hudson-Hunslet 20 hp diesel locomotive of 4-4-0 steam outline, together with five closed and 10 open 4-wheeled coaches. These were supplied by the Kent & Sussex Woodcraft Ltd firm of Ashford, Kent (Kenex Coachworks), and were finished in a red and cream livery. Each was 9 ft long by 4 ft wide and seated 12 passengers while a further 10 could be accommodated in the 'tender' behind the driver. The maximum speed of the locomotive was 7 mph.

In 1953 the line underwent its next, major change when the entire stock was replaced. Two new diesel-powered cars were built for the line by the Lakeside Miniature Railway, together with one closed and four open trailers. These seven bogie vehicles were operated as one rake in the following order (from the pier head end): motor car, closed trailer, open trailers, motor car. The livery scheme was one of blue and silver - the Corporation finally having realised its desired silver effect after some 17 years! - and the train was christened with champagne in July that year as the 'Silver Belle' by a former town councillor, Mrs Mae Bamber. The line itself

The *Silver Belle* crossing the boating lake on the reclaimed land between the shore station and the sea . . .   *C.H. Loker*

. . . and at the pier head terminus.   *C.H. Loker*

was officially referred to as the Southport Pier Miniature Railway. In the summer a frequent service was provided from 9 am to 10.30 pm daily whilst the winter service operated on Fridays, Saturdays and Sundays only.

In the summer of 1970 the line was affected by a serious derailment which badly damaged both train and track, putting the line out of action for the rest of the season. That December it was announced by the Chairman of the town's Publicity & Attractions Committee that the 'Silver Belle' was at the end of her working life and would therefore not be repaired. It was also stated that the pier concession holders (Fortes) were studying two possibilities. One was to provide new stock for the line and repair the existing track; the other was to replace the railway entirely with a pneumatically-tyred vehicle running in a guideway (for which interesting, though ill-fated precedent, see Chapter Nine). The fact that the train's engines were still in working order seems to have influenced the final decision, for on 18th March, 1971 it was decided to run a shortened train on the repaired track for that summer season pending a later decision on the eventual future of the line. Only three open coaches were now used between the two motor cars, the closed carriage and the other two open ones, both damaged in the accident, having been sold in 1970 to the 2 ft gauge West Lancashire Light Railway close by at Hesketh Bank. (There they were renumbered 12 and 13 as passenger carriages hauled behind one of this enthusiast-operated line's locomotives.)

By 1972 however it had been decided to restock the line and services recommenced the following Easter with a new train: a Bo-Bo diesel hydraulic locomotive named *English Rose* with a Ford 2711 engine (Works No. 23/1973) hauling three open and one closed bogie carriages, all from Severn-Lamb Ltd of Stratford-upon-Avon. The closed carriage at the landward end of the rake was a driving trailer with its leading bogie powered via an hydraulic pipe from the locomotive at the other end of the rake. About 100 passengers could be seated in the train. Livery was maroon. Services ceased that November for the winter so that two new bridge sections of the pier could be installed over the Marine Drive, Southport pier being unusual in that much of it actually extends over (mainly reclaimed) land in the form of pleasure gardens.

Latterly the train driver collected passengers' fares following the closure of the toll booth at the landward end of the railway; in 1996 a return fare of 80p was charged during the day but only 35p in the evening (with the railway open from 10.00 am to 11.00 pm).

Following a short period of closure of the railway in the mid-1990s it was reported in 1996 (when services recommenced to mark The Year of the Pier) that the pier's structure was seriously degraded and it faced closure within two years if not repaired. The railway (and much of the pier) closed in 1998 and the stock was sold. Thankfully, that same year the National Heritage Lottery Fund awarded £1.7 million to the Southport Pier Trust towards the estimated £2.3 million cost of refurbishing this Grade II listed structure. Plans for the work, scheduled to begin in September 1999, provide for a new railway, though the exact form it will take is as yet unknown.

An Edwardian postcard showing the Walton-on-the-Naze pier railway's three Ashbury cars; one of the trailers (emblazoned COAST DEVELOPMENT COMPANY LTD) is apparently being used as a shelter. The number of steamers by the pier head indicates just how important this traffic was.   *Author's Collection*

A later Edwardian postcard showing a more deserted (off-season?) pier with only the motor car in use. Note the new entrance structure.   *Author's Collection*

Chapter Nine

Walton-on-the Naze Pier Railways

The first pier to be built at Walton-on-the-Naze in Essex (or Walton-le-Soken as it was once called) was opened in 1830; it was a wooden structure some 300 ft in length, subsequently extended to 800 ft.

In August 1898 a new pier was opened on the site of the old one as the result of a scheme promoted by the Walton-on-the-Naze Pier & Hotel Co. Ltd (and authorised by the Walton-on-the-Naze Pier Order 1897). During construction, however, this company became incorporated into the Coast Development Co. Ltd (*see Chapter Two*), under whose ownership the new structure was opened. The pier was 2,600 ft long and included a single-track electric railway of 3 ft 6 in. gauge running the length of the north side to the south-curving pier head. The line was laid with 36 lb. rails and, unusually for a pier railway, the current (fed from a 50 kw Parker generator) was supplied from a centre rail rather than from one beside the track.

Rolling stock consisted of a motor car and two trailers, all open-sided cross-bench cars built by the Ashbury Railway Carriage & Iron Co. Ltd of Manchester and mounted on Peckham trucks; the motor car's truck was equipped with two Crompton 15 hp motors. All three carriages (each seating 32 passengers) normally ran coupled together as a unit, though the line's one siding at the pier head was probably used to store one or both of the trailers if traffic was light. A second, identical set of cars also ran on the line though whether these dated from 1898 or 1904 is not certain.

The railway lasted until the end of the 1935 summer season, when it was closed and lifted, and was replaced by an unusual - if not unique - system of transport which opened to the public the following year. A 6 ft-wide trough formed by narrow timber baulking fixed vertically to the decking provided a guide-way for a single battery-powered carriage. Built by Electricars Ltd, this ran on six wheels and was fitted with toast-rack seating for 20 passengers. The wheels - two to each axle - were equipped with pneumatic tyres and the centre axle was driven by a small electric motor. Horizontal guiding wheels ran along the sides of the trough and 'steered' the car along the pier. Conventional steering gear was in fact incorporated into the car for possible road use but kept locked whilst it was in the trough. The car could be driven from either end with the drum-type controllers and foot-brakes supplied, thus doing away with any need to turn it round at the end of its journey.

In 1937 the pier (and battery car) were purchased by the New Walton Pier Co. and the service remained unchanged until Saturday 30th May, 1942 when both were destroyed by fire (thus pre-empting any decision by the authorities to breach the pier). After the war however the pier was rebuilt by Walton-on-the-Naze Urban District Council and during reconstruction a 2 ft gauge contractor's line was laid along its ½ mile length; it re-opened in 1948 in time for the summer season with this line adapted for carrying passengers. Simply laid with light, flat-bottomed rails bolted to wooden sleepers laid directly onto the decking

The electric railway's staff pose for the camera at the shore station where a slight curvature of the track and platform took the line to the edge of the wider decking here. The leading car has now lost its ownership legend.   *Lens of Sutton*

A postcard of the post-World War II 2 ft gauge railway with disguised Baguley 3024 of 1939 setting off with its three carriages for the pier head. *Author's Collection*

A poor quality, but rare earlier postcard (franked 1st November, 1954) showing the very basic nature of the line at the landward 'station', its loop just long enough for two coaches and the former wooden guide trough just visible in the distance. The message on the card reads: 'The pier is absolutely empty this week. This train is in its shed.' *Author's Collection*

(again along the north side of the pier), it consisted of a single track inside the battery car's old wooden trough with a short siding and run-round loop at the shore end, and a loop and turntable at the pier head.

One engine provided the motive power: an 0-4-0T steam-outline, Ford petrol-engined locomotive built by E.E. Baguley Ltd of Burton-on-Trent, a type the firm supplied to a number of pleasure lines before and after the war. Works No. 3024 of 1939, it came from Wilson's Pleasure Railway at Allhallows-on-Sea in Kent where it had been numbered 1 and given the name *Dreadnought* (dropped at Walton). In 1952 the original engine was replaced by a Lister 24 hp FR2 diesel unit and in 1972 an 18 hp Lister was fitted, whilst a new livery of red and black replaced the former red and white and a 'Thomas the Tank Engine'-style face painted directly onto the smokebox door.

Some mystery surrounds the railway's three open bogie coaches. The accompanying postcard illustration suggests that originally only two were supplied by Baguley (Works Nos. 3025 and 3026); these were later joined by a third Baguley vehicle. Each had six cross-bench tramway-type reversible seats and held 18 passengers and at the same time as the locomotive's repainting their livery was altered from red and white to red and orange. (The locomotive's livery was then modified to match this!) Another change at some stage was the removal of the open framework of their sides. A small 4-wheel flat wagon completed the rolling stock fleet. A charge of 4p during the 1970s permitted access to the pier and/or a ride on what was, despite its gauge, in effect a miniature pleasure railway.

The line operated from Easter to October but fell into disuse after severe storms hit the East Coast on 11th-12th January, 1978 and, although the pier remains open, any hopes of repairing the railway were scotched by further storm damage the following New Year's Eve. After overhaul at Steamtown, Carnforth, the locomotive and coaches saw service at the Camelot Theme Park at Charnock Richard in Lancashire (early 1980s) and at Hewitts Farm at Orpington in Kent (late 1980s) before moving, in 1991, to the Amerton Railway near Stafford where, following another overhaul, the locomotive has been renamed *Dreadnought* and still hauls coaches Nos. 3025 and 3026, plus a third, longer carriage possibly also from Walton.

Chapter Ten

Other Lines

Besides those described in previous chapters, a large number of other lines have existed on Britain's piers. These can be grouped fairly neatly into a number of types, the humblest of which was the hand-worked luggage line which never made the step up to carrying passengers. Usually of narrow gauge to keep the weight of its trucks to a minimum, such lines which survived unaltered into the 20th century were rendered obsolete by the decline in coastal steamer traffic between the two World Wars. Several such tramways are known to have been operated but virtually all have been poorly recorded, the main evidence for their existence being their depiction on maps, postcards or photographs of the period. Three are believed to have been located in North Wales - at Bangor and Beaumaris on opposite sides of the Menai Straits, serving both ferry and coastal steamer passengers, and along the coast to the east at Rhyl - whilst in England examples are known from Sheerness and Deal in Kent, and Minehead and Weston-super-Mare in Somerset. A rare modern example was laid on the jetty at Drake's Island, off Plymouth, probably in the 1970s; the jetty itself was constructed in 1939 and was one of a host of similar lines at defence establishments around the coast of Britain used for the loading/unloading of small but heavy items (e.g. torpedoes) for research or other purposes.

The luggage line on Birnbeck Pier, Weston-super-Mare, c. 1890, with one of the manually-propelled trolleys in use; the (unofficial) passenger is probably a Director of the pier company. The pier opened in 1867 and the tramway in 1884.

Courtesy Woodspring Museum Service

77

An Edwardian postcard of Sheerness Pier with its luggage line to the left and a paddle steamer right.   *Author's Collection*

The luggage line on Sheerness pier as depicted on the 1908 edition Ordnance Survey 6 in. map.

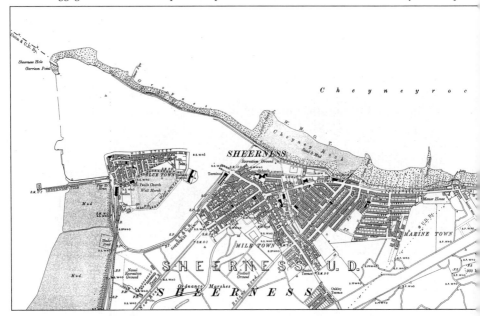

Other goods-only lines have served to transport minerals or other freight from the shore out to waiting cargo boats.   These were simple continuations of industrial lines from quarries or similar sites inland, or goods-only spurs off a major railway such as at Aberdovey on the mid-Wales coast on the Cambrian Railways system.   Allied to these were those railways which were simple continuations of main or branch lines out to pierhead termini for the transhipment of passengers and freight at locations as diverse as the major cross-Channel ports, important estuary crossings such as from Fahen on the Londonderry & Lough Swilly Railway in Ireland, or quiet backwaters like that served by the Kelvedon, Tiptree & Tollesbury Pier Light Railway in Essex.   In truth, there was little to distinguish these types of line from their dock or quayside counterparts other than the fact that they ran out on piers (which often, over the years, were replaced by more substantial stone jetties anyway or, in the case of the branch at New Holland opposite Hull, killed off by the opening of the Humber road bridge).

Tramway systems running onto piers have always been comparatively rare though one of the country's earliest tramways, opened in 1865 by the Landport & Southsea Tramways Co., ran from Portsmouth Town station through the town centre and onto Clarence Pier at Southsea to meet the Isle of Wight ferries. (More famously, Pier Head terminus on Liverpool's tramway network was actually on the Mersey dockside.)

A handful of miniature railways have, at one time or another, been operated on piers. Often lasting a few seasons only - sometimes less - at any one location, the chronicling of such peripatetic lines is notoriously difficult. Examples are known to have been laid on the iron jetty extension at Margate, on Birnbeck Pier at Weston-super-Mare, at Hunstanton, on Lowestoft Claremont Pier, at Herne Bay and at Bognor Regis (as well as on the stone jetties at Margate and Ramsgate).

Finally, in a category all of its own, the Marina Pier at Ramsgate (1881-1930) housed for many years a gentle out and back roller-coaster, or switchback railway, that filled its 550 ft length.

The impressive pre-World War I amusement facilities, lifeboat station and luggage line terminus on the unique island pier head of Birnbeck Pier, Weston-super-Mare.
Author's Collection

Bibliography

General Works
Adamson, Simon H.: *Seaside Piers*, Batsford / Victorian Society, 1977.
Mickleburgh, Timothy J.: *The Guide to British Piers*, Piers Information Bureau, Hebden
Bridge, 3rd ed. 1998.

Blackpool
Orchard, Alison: *Blackpool North Pier Tramway*, Lancastrian Transport Publications,
Blackpool, 1992.

Felixstowe and Walton-on-the-Naze
Anderson, R.C.: *The Tramways of East Anglia*, Light Railway Transport League, 1969.
Anderson, R.C. & Gillham, J.C.: *The Tramways of East Anglia*, Light Rail Transit
Association, (*c*. 1982).

Herne Bay
'INVICTA': The *Tramways of Kent Vol 2: East Kent*, Light Railway Transport
League / Tramway & Light Railway Society, 1975.

Hythe
Stearn, Wm A. & Moody, Bert: *The Hythe-Southampton Ferry*, Eltrac Publications, 2nd ed.
1970.
Titheridge, Alan: *Hythe Pier and Ferry - A History*, Itchen Printers Limited, Southampton,
2nd ed. 1986.

Ramsey
Jones, Norman: *Isle of Man Tramways*, Foxline Publishing, Stockport, 1994.
Pearson, F.K.: *Isle of Man Tramways*, David & Charles, 1970.

Ryde
Blackburn, A. & Mackett, J.: *The Railways and Tramways of Ryde*, Town & Country Press,
Bracknell, 1971.

Southend
Bride, Alderman H.N.: *The Story of Southend Pier*, Corporation of Southend-on-Sea, (*c*. 1950).
Burrows, V.E.: *The Tramways of Southend-on-Sea*, Advertiser Press, Huddersfield, 1965.
Frost, K.A. & Carson, D.J.: *Southend Pier Railway*, Ian Henry Publications, Romford,
2nd ed. 1990.
Herbert, A.P.: *The Battle of the Thames - The War Story of Southend Pier*, County Borough
of Southend-on-Sea, 1945.
Shepherd, E.W.: *The story of Southend Pier. . . and its associations*, Egon Publishers Ltd,
Letchworth, 1979.

Other lines
Croft, D.J.: *A Survey of Seaside Miniature Railways*, The Oakwood Press, 1992.
Ludlam, Alf: *Railways to New Holland and the Humber Ferries*, The Oakwood Press, 1996.
Skidmore, Ian: *Bangor Pier 1896-1988*, Community Task Force, 1988.
Terrell, Stan: *Birnbeck Pier: a short history*, North Somerset Museum Service, no date (1996).
Turner, Keith: *North Wales Tramways*, David & Charles, 1979.

Anyone interested in any aspect of Britain's piers is strongly advised to join the
National Piers Society (Membership Secretary: Phil Johnson, 82 Aldington Close, Lodge
Park, Redditch, Worcs. B98 7NF).
Specialist publications on piers can be obtained from the Piers Information Bureau at 3
Withburn Close, Upton, Wirral L49 6QH.